How to Remember Names & Faces

A Key to Successful Business Relationships

Dr. Jacqueline Albright

How to Remember Names & Faces – A Key to Successful Business Relationships

Copyright © 2019 by Jacqueline Albright

First Edition

Cover art by Alerrandre Rivera

ISBN: 978-0-9860083-0-6

For information about bulk orders, please contact
The Jacqueline Albright Group
Phone: 917-983-6100
Email Jacqueline@supersizedmemory.com
Web: www.jacquelinealbright.com

Library of Congress Catalog Card Number: 9780986008368

Printed in the United States of America

DEDICATION

This book is dedicated to everyone who wants to
easily recall the names of those they meet.

May your journey through this book
bring you great rewards and many successes.

Share its message with your
friends, family coworkers and employees,.

ACKNOWLEGEMENTS

To those who have been an inspiration
and motivating force in my life.

Your wisdom, love and acts of kindness
are the memories I choose to remember
and those I keep close to my heart.

TABLE OF CONTENTS

1 YOU HAVE GREATNESS WITHIN YOU

You're about to embark on a life-changing journey. A journey that will assist with your success and endear you to those you meet. You're about to learn how to remember the names of everyone you meet!

Before I go onstage, I introduce myself to as many people in the audience to get to know their names. We chat for a bit before moving on to another, sometimes being introduced to 3, 4 or more people at a time. Then I walk onstage to explain in one hour, what you're about to savor and drink in at your own leisure.

After the introductions I ask everyone I met to stand up and then sit when I've pointed to them and called out their name. Often an audience of several hundred people stands. One evening I spoke to an audience with a large number of Tom, Tommy and Thomas's in attendance. Some were friends, others were Father and sons and one family had three generations with the name Thomas in the audience. I left them all standing for last and then called them out one after another in succession to great applause.

However, the applause really belonged to the audience and it belongs to you the reader. I'm not doing anything you can't do as well. I applaud you for taking the time to read <u>How to Remember Names and Faces</u> and I applaud you for recognizing how important a tool it is for developing business connections. You are the backbone of the business community. You are the backbone of the job market. You are the backbone of your family's financial stability. Developing this skill will improve your financial and managerial success. A skill that will stay with you for a lifetime once learned.

HARNESS YOUR GREATNESS

You have greatness within you. More Greatness than you even realize. Untapped potentials that lie within you to remember the names and faces of everyone you meet. Untapped potentials this book will unlock and reinforce. I'll show you how. I'll help you tap into that energy. What I do onstage with hundreds of people in an audience.... you can do too.

You do not need to be a genius. You do not need a high IQ. You do not even need a high school education. You simply need the motivation of will and the curtain pulled back to be taught the SECRETS BEHIND THE MAGIC. Once you understand how it works then with practice you'll acquire the same skill to harness this greatness within you too.

Having the ability to Remember Names is the cornerstone for successful business people. To the outsider, it appears as though it's a unique knack, not realizing they too can acquire the same skills. I'm here to reveal those secrets and hold your hand while you take those steps. Steps that won't take any time out of your day to practice. A skill that will accelerate the successes in your business and everyday life.

MY GOAL FOR YOU

My goal for you is your goal as well. It's the reason why you're reading this book and the reason why I went to lengths to make it clear, concise and straightforward to follow. What I want for you is to easily remember the names of everyone you're introduced to at the next conference, networking event, dinner party, barbeque or wedding you attend. My goal for you is to remember the names of every new person you meet in every nook and cranny of your life; from the person who pumps your gas to all the employees who work for you to your kid's school mates and their teachers as well as all your coworkers, managers and executives of your company. You especially want to remember the names of returning clients and their family, your bread and butter, as well as everything else in-between.

Do you want that? Because that was my goal and objective when writing this book and I want it to be your goal as well. It doesn't require having any special education ... only your commitment to use and put into practice the advice you're about to embark upon.

Why am I so passionate about this? Why am I encouraging you to learn how to remember names and faces, especially if you're in business? Because it will change you life, personally and professionally. Don't take my word for it. Read further and you'll begin to understand the why for yourself. When you begin to apply these techniques you'll see the affects amongst your own circle of acquaintances. It will provide you with an ability to develop more lucrative business relationships, opportunities and pipelines.

Send me your success stories and I'll share them with other readers, explaining how remembering someone's name brought you success to: Jacqueline@supersizedmemory.com

MAKE A PROMISE TO PRACTICE

Developing a knack to remember names doesn't happen over night. It takes practice to reinforce your speed and skill. Are you motivated? Are you ready to make a commitment to yourself to reach that goal? Say it with me,

**"I promise myself to
Remember the names of everyone I meet."**

Repeat it Again!

That's what I want for you. It all starts with your will, your motivation and passion to put what you're about to learn into practice.

Just to prove a point, let's say I wrote a book on how to play tennis that explained the strategies of the game. After reading the book would you expect to play tennis as well as Roger Federer or Serena Williams? Me neither.

You have all the tools you'll need in this book and I will guide you step by step through the process. The good thing is, it won't cost you a thing. It won't take any time out of your day, it won't take you away from your work and you won't have to schedule appointments with others to do it. You simply need to use the tools you're about to learn on every person you meet. Whether you meet them in person, see them on TV or view their picture in the newspaper.

Practice simply requires going about your day with an AWARENESS to USE the techniques on everyone in order to *Remember Their Names.* Some days you'll be more successful than others but with time, and often you won't realize it, you'll be able to accomplish what you thought was impossible.

This skill is the cornerstone to developing successful business relationships. Whether you're in corporate, sales or are self-employed, businesses are all dependent upon loyal and repeat customers and it begins by calling them by their name.

There is Greatness Within You and you have the power to untap it! Remembering Names is your key to opening doors to further your business relationships and parlay it into financial success. It's a skill worth learning. Now's the time!

2 THE POWER OF A NAME

I'm often introduced to top producers and executives in their field of sales and business who request I speak to their employees, teams and groups so they too can acquire the skill of remembering client's names. As top producers or owners of a company, they "Get it." They understand how important it is to call someone by their name and/or title to reinforce their business connections and to develop new ones. They're the ones cheering-on their staff and encouraging them to expand their memory skills, knowing how integral it is to their success.

WHY NAMES ARE IMPORTANT

There is POWER in calling someone by name. Powerful enough that you should know someone's name isn't just a name.[1] It represents their IDENTITY and is a composite of WHO THEY ARE! Where they've been, where they currently are in their life, where they're going and who they will become. [2]

A person's name represents their EGO.
A person's name encompasses their identity and personality,
A person's name epitomizes their psyche, their ethos and their self-pride.

When you take the time to remember someone's name, it conveys to them that you RESPECT them. It expresses that you CARE ENOUGH to remember. That you VALUE them, that you SEE them and that they're NOT INVISIBILE to you. It creates an opportunity to feel more CONNECTED to you, more LOYAL to you, which opens the doors to new relationships and potentially new prospective clients.

A famous quote by an Anonymous author said:

**"People will forget what you said.
People will forget what you did.
But people will never forget
How you made them feel."**

How we make others FEEL lingers in their memories of us. Remembering someone's name forges a feeling that will create a lasting first impression that says I RESPECT you, I VALUE you and I CARE ENOUGH to recognize your individual identity. These are the ingredients to developing LOYAL relationships with your customers and the people you meet in your everyday life, from the waiter and supermarket cashier to the upper management persons of your company. They could all become future clients or know someone who could. That's why acquiring the ability to remember names is a cornerstone skill used by successful business people.

Shakespeare famously wrote in *Romeo & Juliet*,

"What's in a name?
That which we call a rose by any other name
Would smell as sweet."

Juliet said this to Romeo as she argued that it didn't matter to her that his last name was Montague, her family's arch rival. However, most of us are familiar enough with the story to know just how much it mattered to Juliet's family, the Capulet's that Romeo was a Montague.

According to Juliet's admission, an actual rose could be called a spoon or anything you wish and it would still smell as sweet as a rose but realistically, you can't call a woman named Rose by any other name without insulting her and making yourself look smaller in her eyes. We do not go by other names regardless of how sweet we are because our names are connected to our ego, our personalities, our individualities, our identities and our family history. It's all encapsulated in our name. When you call someone by their name it tells them YOU SEE THEM, YOU

RESPECT THEM. As a result, they're more likely to connect to you, which is the key to opening the doors to business relationships

Dale Carnegie, the author of *"How to Win Friends and Influence People"*, said:

"Someone's name is the sweetest word TO THEM in any language."

He repeatedly emphasized in his book and business courses how important it was to learn the art of remembering names to open new doors to business relationships. Written in 1936 and selling over 30 million copies world-wide, Mr. Carnegie's advice is as true today as it was then.

Let me share with you a real life example of an event that demonstrates just how POWERFUL remembering names is and the consequences that can occur if you forget a name.

It happened toward the end of 2017, when rebels in Niger killed four soldiers. Several days later, the President called one of the wives of the fallen soldiers to offer his condolences, which provoked a scathing rebuke in an interview on *Good Morning America* by the Widow Myeshia Johnson, whose husband Sgt. La David Johnson had been killed in the attack. Myeshia said she was very upset with the president and explained, in her own words his conversation, while holding back tears:

"The President struggled to remember my husband's name. I heard him stumbling on it and trying to remember his name and that's what hurt me the most, because if my husband is out there fighting for our country and he risked his life for our country, why can't you remember his name? That's what made me upset and cry even more because my husband was an awesome soldier!" [3]

She continued to explain that the President said he had her husband's file on his desk, which he referred to before stumbling through her husband's name - Sgt. La David Johnson.

Viewers of the interview could see that Myeshia was both emotionally and physically upset as she relayed her story to George Stephanopoulos and the world that the President couldn't remember her husband's name. That her husband's name wasn't on the tip of the President's tongue. That the President admitted he had to read it from a chart, leaving her feeling as though he didn't appreciate her or her husband's sacrifice to protect our country from terrorists.

This is just one example of many demonstrating HOW POWERFUL remember names is to developing long-term relationships. Using and reciting someone's name "off the tip of your tongue" shows respect, shows concern, demonstrates you care and helps to forge relationships with people you don't even know that can mushroom into loyal connections.

The President lost an opportunity to create a bond with Myeshia and her family during his call. In addition, her anguish and feelings of disrespect were also heard and seen by entire groups of people, especially the African American and the Gold Star Communities. He lost an opportunity to create a loyal relationship with Myeshia Johnson and the community she represents. Then the unexpected happened, which further affected the image of the President. Her interview went VIRAL and was talked about on news channels and the Internet worldwide for days.

Looking forward into the future, when reporters check in on Myeshia and how she and her family are doing at the one year anniversary, at the 5 year anniversary or if she writes a book about her husband, she will again and again explain how she, her family and her community were made to feel disrespected and dishonored because the President couldn't remember her husband's name Sgt. La David Johnson.

The President was probably surprised to have heard about her reaction and the hoopla it created in the news. It was a condolence call after all and he denied having forgotten his name. What he really failed to understand was the POWER behind remembering someone's name and to have it roll off your tongue to convey honor and respect. It's a lesson to us all.

Here's another example most of you are familiar with that demonstrates the POWER of using someone's name and the consequences it can have on our intimate relationships.

If comes from the forth season finale of the TV series F-R-I-E-N-D-S when Ross and Emily are about to be married in England. The romantic scene was set in a war-torn building transformed into a dreamy wedding venue. As Emily and Ross stood before each other, witnessed by their friends and family to vow their eternal love and commitment, Ross accidently says, "I Ross, take thee Rachel." The camera zoomed in on the reactive expression of Ross's ex-girlfriend Rachel, then on his soon to be wife Emily, while the TV audience gasped in surprise. Although they did get married, Emily remained forever suspicious of his feelings for Rachel, which tainted their marriage and led to their separation in the next season.

For all the reasons explained above, remembering your future spouse's name while exchanging vows or saying their name when being intimate conveys more power than you realize and can have a strong influence on your partner's ability to trust your love for them. It recognizes their identity and who they are. As Dale Carnegie said, "Someone's name is the sweetest word TO THEM in any language." There's POWER in using a name and learning how to harness that power is what you're about to learn!

3 REMEMBERING NAMES IMPROVES YOUR BUSINESS

Motivational Speaker Zig Ziglar preached to his audiences the following sentiment:

> *"People don't care how much you know
> Until they first know how much you care."*

Motivational speaker Bob Burg called the following statement "The Golden Rule of Sales":

> *"All things being equal, people will do business
> with, and refer business to those people
> they know, like and trust."*

Names are the KEY to developing relationships that will get people to know, like and trust you and remembering someone's name conveys that you care. It's the foot in the door if you like and one of the reasons why individuals "drop names" to sway and inspire confidence and credibility to others. Let me show you how to build your own key that will swing open those doors leading to future business.

It probably wouldn't surprise you when I confess that I ask everyone I meet for their name saying,

> *"I DIDN'T GET YOUR NAME."*

Most of the time they never offered it and sometimes they'll say just that before telling it to me. It's out of sheer preference that I pose a statement rather than asking, "What's your name?"

After they tell me, I extend my hand to shake theirs saying, "Hi, I'm Jacqueline," and if I don't shake their hand I at least make *EYE CONTACT* with them when I introduce myself.

Days, weeks or months later when I walk into their shop, gas station or restaurant I enthusiastically call them by name saying, **_"It's good to see you!"_** The first time I do that they have a look of surprise and confusion on their face as though saying, "How do I know you?" This is especially true when people feel invisible in their job. You know who those are; people who serve and take care of your needs every day but rarely get attention or recognition for their work and assistance. The barrister at Starbucks, the cashier at the grocer, the shampoo person at your hair salon, the nurses at the doctor's office, your postal deliverer and many, many more that you interact with on a regular basis but didn't think to ask their name.

The point is, you open doors to developing relationships with everyone you meet when you show them the respect of asking for and remembering their name. It conveys that you see them, you recognize them and you appreciate what they do. Let me reinforce, this isn't a relationship that goes beyond whatever facility they work for but instead one based on courtesy and acknowledgment. When you walk up to a person and call them by their name, when they're "invisible" to others, you WILL stand out amongst the crowd. It has been my experience that when people feel recognized they'll go out their way to help you.

HIT THE LIKE BUTTON

We live in a Facebook culture where people want to be recognized and SEEN through their downloaded pictures, videos and details of what they're doing every day. They want their friends to WATCH THEM, to LIKE THEM and to COMMENT. When their friends hit the LIKE button, it tells them that they matter, their pictures matter, what they've done and said matters. [1]

Neurologists have found that "Being Liked" on Facebook creates a secretion of feel good chemicals in the brain called <u>dopamine & endorphins</u> that control the brain's reward and pleasure centers. Dr. Emily Deans, explained in an article in <u>Psychology</u>

<u>Today</u> that "Dopamine enables us to not only seek out rewards but to take action to move toward them again and again."[2]   In the same light, when you call someone by name – their favorite word in any language - you're telling them that THEY MATTER. It's as though you're hitting the LIKE button, giving them a shot of dopamine – the "Feel Good Chemical."   In essence you're developing a relationship whereby they feel good every time you call them by name, every time you meet.

You're only now beginning to understand why using someone's name is so POWERFUL. It's especially important in building businesses that are dependent on repeat and loyal customers: restaurants, salons, mechanic shops, accountants, doctors, lawyers, realtors, sales people, stockbrokers or negotiating corporate or government contracts – to name a few.

CREATING BIRD DOGS

Motivational speaker Bob Burg professed,

"People ultimately choose to do business With people they like, know and trust."

They prefer to buy from their friends or people they have an association with, even if it is only based on multiple one-minute encounters at an office or store. [3] Once the door is open, then you can start working to develop a trust and value that extends into a future business relationship.

Here's how I go about doing just that:

 I make it a habit to ask everyone I meet, everywhere I go, for their name whenever possible. The next time I see them I say, "Hi Jerry," and either go about my shopping or take a minute or less to exchange a few words.   After a few contacts, I'm comfortable enough to say, "Hi Jerry. Good to see you." Then I give them a business card saying, "Jerry, I'm a professional speaker on the topic of *How to Remember Names & Faces*. If you know of anyone who's in need of a speaker for an event, could you pass them my card? I'll make sure they have an exceptional experience that will boost their business." I leave it at that unless they ask me questions but usually I continue with my shopping.

This works for any business you're in; if you own a bakery, work as doctor, accountant, sell or fix cars, own a florist, a pharmacy or run a gym – anything! Here's a sample script you can use. Feel free to modify it if you choose:

"Hi (Add Name), I'm a (Add Business Affiliation here).

Let me give you my business card.
If you, your friends or family ever need my services (Want to buy a car, buy or sell real estate, need a cake, are interested in growing their finances or want to eat at the best restaurant in town) have them call me personally and I'll take good care of them."

If you choose to give a discount or any other incentive such as 5% - 10% off, this would be the time to do it. For example you could say, "If anyone you know is interested in buying a car, have them call me personally and I'll give them a discount plus the best service to help them find their dream automobile."

You have just created a **Bird Dog**, someone who can introduce your business to an entire circle of people you don't know and may not have access to. A group of family and friends who trust this individual and may consider their recommendation when offered. From there, everywhere you go, every business you visit or shop in, everyone you've taken the time to remember and called by name you can offer your card, creating multiple Bird Dogs all over town and everywhere you travel. I have personally spoken at several events traced back to people I casually got to know and offered a card to.

ONE LAST THING - It goes without saying that you need to say what you mean and follow up with what you say. I was raised with old fashion values that believed your word was your bond. My Grandmother would often tell my brothers and me, "If all you do is clean toilets, then be the best toilet washer you can be." The point was made clear: Keep your word and do a better than average job. I'm advocating that you too take this powerful tool and provide your best service to those you meet; to follow through, keep your word and offer great service.

WHY TITLES ARE IMPORTANT

When I practiced in Queens, New York Derek Jeter was a local hero. A NY Yankee shortstop who was a 5 times World Series Champion, a 14 times All-Star player and the captain of his team for 11 years. Despite all the awards and successes in his career I always admired him for his outward demonstration of respect for Yankee Manager Joe Torre. Derek always called him Mr. Torre whenever he referred to him in person or during interviews.

In an interview with the Yankee's Manager, he was asked about this and explained that he told Derek many times to call him Joe but Derek insisted it wasn't right. My patients, baseball fans through and through, held him in even higher esteem for this small but powerful gesture. To them it conveyed respect to the Yankee franchise and the city of New York where Derek was a role model for their kids. Parents often referred to his behavior as an example of how to treat others. Too them he was a winner on and off the field.

The point of this story is to demonstrate Derek's ability to win over a city. Not just baseball fans but everyone from young to old whether they followed the Yankees or not because he cultivated a relationship with others based on respect. Even patients who were avid Met fans, archrivals of the Yankees, only had nice things to say about Derek and may have secretly longed for him to wear the Met's jersey. For me, despite his overwhelming success as a baseball player it was the day he insisted on calling Joe Torre, Mr. Torre that won me over.

In an interview with the NY Post Mr. Torre said, "I think the respect that he's garnered all over the place ... I hear people say, 'I'm not a Yankee fan, but you really have to admire what Jeter's done all these years.' " [3]

In another article with the NY Times, Joe said, "All that 'Mr. Torre' stuff doesn't bother me, but it bothers my wife," the 57-year-old manager was saying with a laugh. "She's a lot younger than I am, and he calls her Mrs. Torre. Maybe that old-fashioned respect explains Derek Jeter better than any of his hitting stats or fielding gems." [4 & 5]

Lets contrast Jeter's insistence to call Joe - Mr. Torres, to the President's faux pas of forgetting a fallen soldier's name and the aftermath with his wife Myeshia Johnson, her family and community. Who do you want to be remembered as?

I can't emphasize enough that a name may seem small and obscure yet taking the time to remember someone's name translates into hitting the LIKE button. A KEY that opens doors to relationships and future successes. If you're reading this book, you're probably a role model in your community; someone who people look up to. What better way of expressing your appreciation and loyalty to them than to call out their name when they walk into your restaurant, shop or place of work.

AVOID GENERIC NAMES

Before ending this chapter, let me finish with this: Whether you're in business or not, don't even think of calling someone a crude and tacky name like Honey, Babe, Doll, Kid, Guy or Dude unless they're family, you work for a surf shop or you're talking to animals. It's the LAZY PERSON'S shortcut to avoid remembering names.

Generic names can make people feel offended, unimportant and disrespected. Even though they may not tell you it bother them it conveys you don't think they're worth your time because they're beneath you. It reminds me of the *GREY'S ANATOMY* character Dr. Christina Yang who called her residents One, Two, Three and Four for a whole season, conveying that they were nobodies and not worth her recognition.

Although I've met many successful people through the years who refer to others by these and other names, could you imagine the potential they could have unleashed and the opportunities they may have missed if they had simply taken the time to learn people's names?

4 WHY WE FORGET NAMES

Do you forget names? If you're reading this because you can "NEVER REMEMBER" someone's name and believe you have a terrible memory, you should be comforted to know that you are in very good company. Everywhere I go executives, sales people and their colleagues tell me they have the worst memory, complaining they always forget names and have experienced more than one embarrassing moment because of it. "I recognize faces," they tell me. I know who they are but their name just escapes me."

Susan attended a presentation I gave and told me this story:

She worked as a mid-level manager of a woman's clothing company with over 200 employees at her location. She only met the CEO of the company once before when they exchanged names. A year later at the end of a meeting, the CEO came off the stage and shook hands with a few employees. She explained, "As he shook my hand, he looked me in the eye and called me by my name, thanking me for my work with the company. I'll never forget how special I felt." She was extremely impressed by "his ability to remember all those employees' names," and when she heard of my lecture on Remembering Names, she made it a point to be there to learn those secrets for herself.

In general, people have trouble remembering names. It's such a common problem that national news outlets and have written on the topic over and over again; from The Wall Street Journal to The NY Times, Forbes Magazine to Inc. Magazine and many more have written dozens of articles on the topic. Inc. Magazine alone published 9 different articles by 9 different authors on

How to Remember Names between 2014 and 2017. That's two articles a year, every year from one business magazine. It's a pervasive problem in the business world and a frequently asked question by their readers. So, if you have trouble remembering names, don't beat yourself up. You are not alone. After reading this book you will know how to remember the names of everyone you meet.

WHY WE FORGET NAMES

Have you ever used your hands to drink water? Maybe a glass wasn't available or you were lakeside camping. Our hands can hold water for a short time and a short distance. We can bring it to our lips, splash it on our face, scoop it into a glass but you can't run across the street with a handful of water and expect to have much left afterwards. In the same way, it's not uncommon to remember someone's name while in their company and then forget it afterwards – sometimes RIGHT after. Their fading name from our memory is similar to water slipping through our fingers.

Here's the actual reason why we forget names:

Names are difficult to remember because they're

> ABSTACT,
>   ETHEREAL and
>   NONCONCRETE.

Most names don't conjure an image for us to SEE in our mind. Like water they're slippery and hard to retain because they're featureless, bland and forgettable. [1] It's like trying to hold onto a breeze. There's no picture for us to create in our mind's eye.

Like water, names are fluid, non-solid and are eventually lost because we're not trained to VISUALIZE names. [2] This is especially true of multisyllabled foreign names, which ZIP right past us like the wind.

TRANSFORMING NAMES

When I was a kid, two of my favorite weekly shows were *I Dream of Jeannie* and *Bewitched*. Actually, in the mid-1960s they were the most watched shows on television. Jeannie was a Persian genie who pranced around in a crop top and harem pants, thought to be risqué for 1960s television and Samantha was a typical suburban housewife and Mother who was secretly a witch with supernatural abilities. Despite their differences in appearance and backgrounds, they had one gift in common. They could both conjure things out of thin air. With the blink of an eye or a twitch of a nose they could transform a man into a frog or relocate you to the moon and back. Like a magician, they could make whatever they thought into a reality.

To begin your journey to remember names, you'll need to think like Jeannie and Samantha. You'll need to conjure solid objects out of thin air. Not in reality but in your mind's eye, to TRANSFORM abstract and nonconcrete names into physical PICTURES that you can see and hold in your thoughts.[3] For example, if you transformed water into ice cubes you could now hold it, carry it long distances and store it forever until you were ready to convert it back into water. You need to transform names in the same way, to make them retrievable when you want to recall them.

Scientific evidence has shown that mental imagery and visualization accelerates learning and improves our brain's ability for long-term memory. Research has shown we can remember more information even faster and for longer periods of time when we think in PICTURES rather than in abstract thought.[4]

Do me a favor, the next time you have a chance, look at the amount of data used by each app on your smart phone. You'll find that photos and videos use over 75% of all your phone's data. Our brain stores information similarly, allocating more of our brain's nerve connections to store pictures rather than abstract thought, but here's the beautiful thing...our brain can just as easily store pictures we SEE IN OUR MIND as it can with our normal sight. It doesn't and can not distinguish between the two and saves them both the same way.[5]

VISUALIZATION

I treated a patient who was a priest at a local University. One day he told me the following story: He attended a university dinner hosted for Coach Phil Jackson, now the most winning coach in basketball history with 11 championship wins. Father sat next to Coach Jackson during dinner giving him a rare opportunity to ask candid questions and listen to stories of basketball's greats. At one point he turned to Phil and asked a question most basketball fans would long to know, "What do you attribute your coaching success to? What would you say is your number one reason for all your wins?"

Phil put down his glass, thought for a second and said, "There are a lot of reasons for both team's successes but if I had to choose one I would say it had to be MENTALLY VISUALIZING MAKING BASKETS. Every day of practice I have the team mentally visualize throwing successful shots; 3-pointers, foul shots, lay-ups, successful passes - over and over again. They're told to hear the swoosh of the ball through the hoop, feel the roar of the crowds and the elation of winning. It's a part of every practice we have."

Coach Jackson's use of visualization for game preparation is an example that he understands how our brains work. He's taking advantage of research proving that our brain cannot distinguish between what it sees with our eyes and what we visualize in our mind.

Seeing names as Mental Pictures
is the most important lesson
you will learn to help you remember names.

Get ready to blink your eyes like Jeannie or twitch your nose like Samantha to conjure images. It will make their name stay with you for a long, long time.

BEFORE WE PROCEED TO THE NEXT CHAPTER

I want to explain that the next two chapters will describe two distinctive methods on How to Remember Names. The first chapter describes a system used by Memory Experts and the second is based on sound advice offered in business, sales and financial magazines as well as national news outlets. Together, these two chapters will fit like a hand in glove with one reinforcing the other to help you acquire the cornerstone business skill to remember the name of every person you meet. Fasten your seats belts ladies and gentlemen. We're about to take off.

5 TO REMEMBER NAMES – CALL A PAL

Welcome to the rest of your new life. You are about to learn how to unleash newfound abilities that will bring successes, alliances and relationships you never thought possible. This chapter is the first part of a two-part system to train your mind to remember names.

We'll start by delving into the most powerful techniques. Techniques used by ALL memory experts and not often written about or explained in business magazines. Techniques that work!

You'll only need to make two small investments that won't cost you a thing. The first is to keep an open mind toward using your *Imagination*. You'll see why as we go along. The second is to commit to *Practice*. That means to practice on everyone you meet. After committing to those two you are ready to begin.

Brace yourself –
What you're about to learn you can't unlearn.

We begin by using the acronym P-P-A-L. Yes, with two Ps.
As you'll also find out, people tend to do extra little things they wouldn't typically do for others because you took the time to remember their name. You want them as your P-P-A-L to facilitate improved relationships with coworkers, bosses, superiors, and casual acquaintances.

P Stands for PAY ATTENTION

The first letter P is the most important of them all. You'll never remember anyone's name unless you take to heart the first letter of the acronym P-P-A-L. Give your book to a friend or colleague if you don't think you can follow the recommendation of this letter or consider it not important. I'll say it again for emphasis: The First letter P of the acronym P-P-A-L is the MOST IMPORTANT step when remembering names and faces. I can't emphasize it enough without banging a pot over your head. Disregard its advice and it will be like going to work without your pants on, fishing without a pole or taking a test without studying. You can go through the motions but you'll never be successful at accomplishing the task.

The first P in P-P-A-L stands for PAY ATTENTION. Blocking out distractions that will compete for your attention and staying focused. It starts with saying to yourself before entering a room, "STAY FOCUSED & GET THEIR NAME." – Repeatedly.

FOCUS STANDS FOR:
FOLLOW–ON–COURSE–UNTIL–SUCCESSFUL

Say it over and over to yourself, "FOCUS & GET THEIR NAME," through the din of the noise; the loud conversations, the background music, the occasional announcements (Let's welcome the bride and groom...), waitstaff interruptions, all while you're being introduced to someone you never met before.

When I first started this training I thought to myself, no problem. I have this. I can do it, easy peasy until reality hit and I found out first hand that it was just the opposite. I was having trouble remembering the names of people I had just been introduced to because I was MORE mentally distracted than I thought I had been.

It wasn't until I fully realized how challenging it was to Pay Attention in a bustling room that I decided to MASTER it once and for all. To this day I still mentally say to myself, "STAY FOCUSED & GET THEIR NAME" whenever I enter a busy room.

You're probably saying to yourself, "Is she kidding? How difficult could it be to hear someone's name? She must be exaggerating!" Well, let's talk about it after your next meeting or get together. When I started, my mind was UNTRAINED and new names simply slipped away. The natural course of learning is to learn from our mistakes. Expect it, then try again and again and again until you can successfully remember everyone's name you just met.

So ask yourself, "How serious are you about learning how to remember the name of every customer that comes into your restaurant, business or store? How serious are you about remembering the names of all your employees, colleagues or students you meet? How serious are you toward building your business and broadening your circle of relationships?" If you resoundingly said, "Jacqueline, I'm VERY Serious. I'm ready to learn, then take PAYING ATTENTION AND STAYING FOCUSED very SERIOUS! Nothing else matters if you don't accomplish this first step.

P Stands for PICTURE

After the pleasantries of shaking hands and exchanging names, the second P of the acronym is activated. This P reminds us to convert their name into a PICTURE.

Not just any picture but a PICTURE you can see in your mind's eye to represent that name. This is your opportunity to become a magician, like Jeannie and Samantha, conjuring objects out of thin air to transform an abstract name into a realistic image of your choice. Like converting water into ice, an image your memory can use to HOLD their name in your memory for a long time.

Transforming names into pictures takes PRACTICE and IMAGINATION but in no time you'll be converting names into images just like a memory expert.

For example, when I hear the name Michael or Mike I see in my mind MICROPHONES – getting mic'd up or standing in front of a group of reporter's microphones. Every time I meet a Joe or Joseph I immediately convert their name into a steaming cup of coffee, otherwise known as a CUP OF JOE. Use images you're comfortable with, whether it's a Starbucks Coffee or coffee in your favorite mug. It's your image and you're more likely to remember it when it's personal and relatable to yourself.

The name Frank I immediately convert into FRANKFURTERS on a grill. Some of you may think of Oscar Myers Frankfurters, Nathan's Frankfurters or even the boiled frankfurters sold at Costco. Again, use the best image of a frankfurter that has an emotional connection to you.

The names Marie and Mary I transform into MARRY or a woman getting MARRIED. I see a bride wearing a long white gown, carrying a bouquet of flowers. I'll even hear the wedding march in my mind.

When I meet someone named Marty or Martin I immediately transform their name into a picture of a MARTIAN – a little grey alien with long fingers.

In Chapter 10 I've provided you with a list of common and not so common names and the images I use for their picture conversion. Use this list as a guide but feel free to create your own images that resonate with your past experiences; for example, some memory experts convert the name Steve into a stove. Instead, I prefer to convert Steve into SLEEVES that flap in the wind like inflated balloons at an auto dealer. Go through the list and personalize those you have an immediate, sentimental connection. It could be from a past memory or even from an event you heard or read about. Having an emotional connection with your image is the best kind of image to create for a name in order to remember it.

Jean is an easy name to visualize. When you hear the name Jean/Gene you immediately think of a pair of blue jeans. What type of jeans you SEE is completely up to you, whether they're low riders, mom jeans, Jordash, Levi's or jeans with rips at the knees. Make them a pair you're likely to remember. When someone has the name Sandy, I think of sand at the beach. For the name MARIA I see a pitcher of SANGRIA. For the name MICHELLE I see a MIT catching SHELLS instead of baseballs. For the name TOM I see DRUMS, often referred to as TOM TOMS. For the name HERB I see a small HERB GARDEN on my windowsill. For the name Roxanne I see a ROCK. It's not necessary to translate their entire name into a picture. An image of only part of their name can act as a trigger and reminder.

Every person I meet named Paul is converted to a basketball, shooting hoops or taking layups. It also works in reverse. Anytime I see a basketball I also think of Paul.

For the name Anna I think of banana but I see ANTS when I hear the name Ann. For the name Evan I see an oven and for the name Karen I see carrots. When I meet someone named Jenny, Jen or Jennifer I see GEMS such as rubies, diamonds and emeralds. For the name Jan or Janice I see JAM spread on toast. For the name Chris or Christopher I see crosses. For the name Allen I see an Allen Wrench and when I meet a Philip I see a Philip screwdriver.

IT'S ALL ABOUT HOW IT SOUNDS

The pictures I create in my mind are based on how the name sounds and not on how it's spelt. If their name is spelt JEAN but they pronounce it JOHN like actor Jean Van Damme, then I'll create a picture for JOHN, which is a toilet "GOING TO THE JOHN" instead of a pair of blue jeans.

VISUALIZE IN DETAIL & USE YOUR 5 SENSES

If someone's name is Ron I transform it into RUM but not just any RUM. I see Captain Morgan with his foot raised on a keg of rum, wearing a long red coat and a pirate's tricorn hat. I try to give the picture as much context and sensory points as I can, whether it means smelling the frankfurters roasting on a grill or hearing the deep laughter of a swashbuckling pirate swigging rum. The extra sensory points help to push their name from short-term memory into long-term memory. Every sensory context you can experience adds more brain neurons into the picture. It's like an investigator's board with red string connecting people, places and things together. It all points to a main person, which in this instance is their name. Having all those sensory reference points create many breadcrumbs you can pull upon when you next meet Ron or Frank in order to remember and call them by name.

Let's go over a few more names; For Elaine I see EATING IN A BOWLING LANE. When I meet someone named Bill I see DOLLAR BILLS, typically a stack of them. For Terry I see a TERRYCLOTH TOWEL. If their name is ROB I see a ROBE but if they introduce themselves to me as ROBERT then I see a ROBOT. Someone with the name Fran, Francine, Frances or Franny I think of France and I see the EIFFEL TOWER.

DEVELOPING NEW HABITS

Now it's time for you to practice. From here on you'll convert every person's name you meet into a picture. Write it down in the space provided for you at the end of the book. You'll use the same image on everyone you meet with that name. Here's an effective plan to quickly convert and transform as many names as possible:

> *First,* start with the people you know, beginning with your immediate family: spouse, children, siblings, parents, grandparents, aunts, uncles, cousins etc.

> *Second*, branch out to neighbors and friends you know or speak to on a regular basis, including those in a local club, group, or organization you belong to outside of work.

> *Third,* proceed to coworkers, bosses, people you know at work including those you don't directly work with but

interact with regularly; such as the cafeteria servers, the barista at your local Starbucks, the kid who makes deliveries to your office when you're too busy to go yourself, your coworker's secretaries and assistants etc.

Forth, after going through the above three steps now work on the names of your favorite TV show characters and news anchors. This step also includes real life people you see on news or talk shows. Can you come up with a picture for Hoda Kotb, host of the 'Today' show with Savannah Guthrie? I visualize a HOLD UP with her arms in the air as a robber takes a wallet. Hold Up is the trigger that will remind me of the name HODA.

To review, when you're at an event ignore distractions, stay focused on your goal to "Get their name" and IMMEDIATELY convert it into a picture.

Keep practicing on everyone you meet and you'll be well on your way to acquiring this cornerstone business skill. Like muscle strengthening, it takes repetition.

TRANSFORMING A NAME INTO PEOPLE YOU KNOW

There are two ways to convert names into pictures. You can convert them into an actual physical object, as described above OR you can convert their name into a PERSON you're very familiar with, who's also called by that name.

Let's use the name JIM as an example. You can convert JIM into a physical object such as a bar bell to represent working out at a GYM or you can think of someone you're familiar with whose name is Jim such as a close friend, relative or a famous person. Two men that come to mind are talk show host Jimmy Fallon and singer Jimmy Buffet. If they don't work for you there are famous people in sports, the arts or in your hometown named Jim who you're personally connected to. These are individuals who can provide you with a depth of "color" to that particular name. Maybe your Father's name is Jim. If you want to use that association, then every Jim you meet you'll associate with your Father.

Every Bruce I meet I associate with Bruce Springsteen wearing a bandana around his head, a sleeveless denim shirt and jeans with a guitar around his neck. I hear the song, "Born in the USA" in my mind and "see" the crowds cheering wildly. How about associating Dolly Parton with every Dolly you meet. When I meet someone named Brittany I associate them with Brittany Spears and hear the song, "Oops, I Did it Again" in my mind. Perhaps you have an aunt Brittany or an uncle Bruce who you have a personal connection to or a close friend named Dolly or Jim; choose them instead by visualizing their clothes or their unique characteristic to associate with the person you're meeting.

When I meet someone named Eva I think of the actress Eva Gabor who starred in the 1970s TV show Green Acres. I hear her saying DAAARRRLING in her unique Eastern European accent as she milks cows in a ball gown and diamond rings. For anyone not familiar with the show, her character was based on an eccentric, socialite who moved to the "country life" from New York City. She resists her new environment every step of the way and regularly tries to convince her husband to return to the city by not dressing for the farm. Eva Gabor's antics on the show have given me much to remember about the name Eva. In essence, instead of conjuring up an object, I'm conjuring a person who I can contextualize with personality, attitude, style of dress and action.

Another name with the same context is the name Rocky from the Rocky Balboa movies. In my mind I clearly see him dodging and weaving in a ring, throwing punches at his opponent, blood dripping from above one eye and calling out Aaadriaan! There's a lot of personality to work with in his character, making it easy to create an image for the name Rocky.

If you used Jimmy Buffett as your go-to person to associate with every JIM you meet, you could see a guy in shorts, flip-flops and a Hawaiian shirt, sipping a margarita with a guitar in his lap. You could also hear in your mind the song Margaritaville – "Wasted away again in Margaritaville; Searchin' for my lost shaker of salt."

When I meet someone named Kate I immediately see a GATE. On the other hand, if your Mother's name is Kate, you may decide that every Kate you meet will be associated with your Mother. When using a person, I suggest you pick an object or action that represents their passion or unique makeup of who they are. For example, if your Mother Kate was a painter, conjure up the image of a paintbrush, canvas or even mentally see your Mother painting. If cooking was her passion then every Kate you meet could evoke an image of your Mother in an apron, using a skillet to prepare the meal you loved the most. See that meal in your mind and mentally imagine yourself smelling it and tasting it. YUM – I'm getting hungry!

Associating a name to a person you know is easier to see in your mind's eye when you have a full understanding of their unique personality quirks and characteristics. Here's another example: When you meet someone named Jean or Gene you can convert their name into a pair of BLUE JEANS or you can see GENE SIMMONS from the band KISS, painted in black and white face paint and his tongue sticking out. You could mentally see pyrotechnic fireworks going off behind him and hear the high note of an electric guitar. If Gene Simmons doesn't work for you then you could certainly use any relative or friend you're familiar with named Jean/Gene, as long as you have an intimate knowledge of what makes them unique that can be translated into a distinctive mental image.

Now that you understand this concept, I feel confident that you'll know what to do if you ever meet someone named Cher. You would have a category of images to choose from; either Cher the singer, Cher the wife of Sonny Bono, Cher the Mother to Chaz Bono or Cher the actress. Any one of these roles could conjure a memorable image to associate with the person you're meeting named Cher. You could even hear the song, "Do you believe in life after love? I can feel something inside me say...."

L Stands for *LOCATION*

We're going to skip the letter A for the moment and jump over to the letter L, which stands for LOCATION. My Father always told me that LOCATION, LOCATION, LOCATION was the most important part of buying a home. LOCATION is equally important in remembering someone's name. "How's that?" you ask.

Let me describe it this way: When you purchase a painting or have family pictures framed, you probably bang a nail or a hook in the wall to proudly display your new work of art for everyone to see. Memory Experts do the same thing and so will you.

To quickly remember someone's name, bang a MENTAL HOOK on his or her face using a UNIQUE FACIAL FEATURE to hang the picture representing their name:

This guy went a step too far.
I said MENTAL HOOK not an Actual Hook.

Then on these MENTAL HOOKS you'll hang the picture you created for their name.

You get the point.

Mental Hooks are actually UNIQUE FACIAL FEATURES, defined as a characteristic that defines their "Look." A feature that's entirely theirs. Usually I choose the first one that stands out to me when we initially meet. It will most likely still be the feature that stands out to me when I meet them next.

Your goal is to QUICKLY identify their UNIQUE FACIAL FEATURE (UFF) with a glance and not a stare.

To help you identify them, here's a list to be on the look out for:

> Deep horizontal lines on their forehead
> Distinctive Lines around their eyes or nose
> Eyebrow Shape (Bushy, Thin, Arched etc.)
> Eyes (Close, Crossed, Almond shaped, Bulging)
> Bags under the Eyes
> Lip Shapes (Full, Thin, narrow, hair lip etc.)
> Scars
> Moles
> Freckles
> Nose Shape (Wide, narrow, upturned, with a bump etc.)
> Chin Shape (Cleft, Squared, Pointy etc.)
> Jutting Jawline
> High Cheek Bones
> Facial Hair such as a beard, goatee, side burns, mustache
>   (Light scruff from not shaving doesn't count.
>   It may not be there the next time you meet.)
> Receding Hairline Patterns (They come in many shapes.)
> Unique Hair style or Color
> Baldness
> Flared ears
> Long Ear lobes
> Neck Waddle
> Eyeglasses

Let's review a few faces and identify their Unique Facial Features together. We'll begin with a face that has exaggerated features then work our way through more "ordinary" ones:

When I quickly scan this face, the first feature that POPS out to me is his big, flared ears. They remind me of Dumbo the elephant whose ears were so big he could fly. Then I notice his pointed, cleft chin, pencil thin lips, high arched eyebrows and wide nose. Any one of those features would work but I usually choose the first distinctive feature that catches my attention.

The first feature I notice is her eyeglasses. To me, they appear to dominate her face. She also has a full bottom lip, arched eyebrows, (although they're partially obstructed by her glasses) and a hair-part on her right.

I immediately notice his facial hair: a well-trimmed beard and mustache.

His hairline goes straight across his forehead, his nose is wide, lips are full and his eyebrows are short. They don't extend past his eyes.

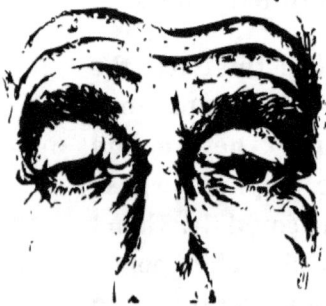

This gentleman's deep, furrowed lines on his forehead is a common Unique Facial Feature. He also has thick, bushy eyebrows.

I notice several UFFs in this young man. The one you choose depends on the feature that catches your attention the most.

I first notice his long, dark, thick eyebrows but his full upper and lower lips come in a close second. He also has distinctively wide eyes that remind me of a Precious Moment's Statue.

The first feature I notice is her very full bottom lip. She also appears to have high cheekbones and a tapered nose and arched eyebrows.

I wouldn't use her hair bun as a feature because she may wear her hair in another style the next time you meet.

There are two features I notice right away: The C-Shaped receding hairline pattern "pops out" as well as a cleft, dimpled chin. He also has prominent ears and a pointed chin. Choose whichever one you notice immediately.

His goatee is the first UFF I notice; especially the way he grooms his chin hair to grow in the middle, up toward the bottom of his lip.

His eyebrows are thin and the area between his brows appears to be groomed or waxed. His hairline has receded back evenly, giving him the appearance of a wide forehead.

Granny has several Unique Facial Features that are characteristic to "Her Look." The most pronounced for me are her Owl-like glasses. She also has a jutting chin and a deep line that extends only from the left side of her nose to her lips.

From time to time you'll be introduced to your client's children or grandchildren. It's equally important to remember their names so you can ask about them when you next meet. Just like adults, you're looking for their UFF. The munchkin on the left has a very full bottom lip and wide eyes.

You should be getting the hang of this. His beard is a blinking light to me and it's the kind of facial characteristic I would notice when I meet him again, (Unless he shaves it off). He also has a squared chin, his ears flare at the top and his eyes are narrow and slit-like.

This gentleman has a distinctive neck waddle, I would use as a UFF. His mustache curls at their ends and his eyes are small and far apart from one another.

This cutie pie has a dimple in his cheek, curly hair and his right ear appears to be flared. His lips are narrow but not unusually thin and his forehead is wide.

When I scan this young man I immediately see his dark, thick eyebrows and jutting chin. He also has a narrow tapered nose.

HAIRLINE PATTERNS

Also used as a location for a Unique Facial Feature:

The **Nixon** hairline pattern has a distinctive M-Shape with a long, central widow's peak.

This **Reagan** hairline has hair higher on one side and a hairline that goes across their forehead.

The **Washington** hairline pattern is bald on top with hair on both sides.

The **Kennedy** hairline is receding on one side with hair fuller and higher on the other side.

Here we see a pronounced triangular shaped hairline pattern on one side only, with their hair swept to the other side, giving the appearance of a wide forehead.

Here's the same pattern as above except reversed. His hair is swept over his forehead, making it less prominent.

Men's Hairline Patterns rarely change, even after decades, unless they're covered with a hairpiece. Women on the other hand can have a variety of looks: hair in a bun, ponytail, swept and wrapped around the back, down and casual, straight, curly or in a bob. I know, I've worn them all. Even a woman with an Afro can wear a wig the next time you meet her or have her hair smoothed down. So I tend not to use a woman's hairstyle as a unique feature unless they're older and have their hair set by a hairdresser weekly. For example, do you remember the show *"The Nanny"* with Fran Drescher? Renée Taylor who played her Mother Sylvia wore the same stiff bouffant for all six seasons. Now that's a hairstyle you can use as a unique facial feature to hang pieces of SILVER on.

The person you're looking at may have flared ears, long earlobes, a tapered or wide nose, full lips, thin lips or a hair lip. Their unique facial feature may be distinctive lines on their face, deep horizontal lines on their forehead or lines on the side of their mouth. It could be a unique hairstyle like Howard Stern's full, long curly locks or Snooki's high poof during her days on *The Jersey Shore*. It could be a unique hair color like the henna blue worn by DNC Chairperson Donna Brazile or the purple hair color worn by Kelly Osbourne.

As an example, I met an advertising executive in New York City who had hair the color of faded red Ralph Lauren shorts. Her name was Carol, which I immediately converted into a picture of Christmas Carolers. Her unique faded red hair made it easier for me to HANG my picture of Christmas Carolers to her "holiday colored" hair. By the way, the next time I saw her had hair the color of faded green but the image of Christmas Carolers in her distinctive hair color had "stuck".

You may also choose the color of their eyes if it captivates their looks. I went to high school with Alec Baldwin's brother Billy who had the most amazing blue eyes. To a 14-year old girl they looked like dreamy blue pools. I'm sure you've met someone with equally memorizing eyes. Eyes you don't want to get caught staring at but eyes you secretly want to stare into for a long time. They're perfect to use as a unique facial feature.

I typically avoid using clothes as a distinguisher because people change their clothes, their ties and their jewelry everyday; however, I will use EYEGLASSES as a UFF because it becomes a part of their "Look." My Grandmother wore glasses that were characteristic of the '60s and '70s and they never changed in my lifetime. My office staff of 8 hardly ever changed their eyeglass style and when they did get new ones, it was similar to their last, just the newest version of their old pair.

Knowing this, when I met a woman at a conference named Cindy, I immediately converted her name into CINDER BLOCKS and choose her rectangle glasses as her unique facial feature to hang her cinder blocks on.

The exception to using eyeglasses is with creative, artistic individuals. Even in their 80s they can change the color and style of their glasses, the color of their hair and in men, the style of their facial hair. From my experience with many artistic patients through the years, colors are meant to be experienced. I had a patient in her mid-70s, sharp as a tack, who came into the office one day with her hair cut short and dyed hot pink. My staff and I were in shock but she loved it and her enthusiasm was contagious. They're in a category of people who like to "Change Up their Look" depending on their mood. When I'm with a group of artistic, individuals, I'm less likely to use their glasses or hair style and instead will choose a UFF strictly on their face.

LET'S RECOUNT

Here's what you'll do when you enter the halls of your next convention where you'll meet people you know and many others you don't:

- Repeat to yourself, "Get their name, get their name" and stay focused against distractions.

A friend comes over to you with someone you've never met and says, "You have to meet Ted!"

- Immediately convert the name TED into a picture of a BED. Contextualize it by choosing the bed you're most familiar with – your personal bed.
- While extending your hand to introduce yourself to Ted: Scan his face to LOCATE a Unique Facial Feature; a mustache, a beard, a scar, a mole, dimples, curved or bushy eyebrows, a cleft chin, rosy cheeks; captivating eye color; distinctive facial lines. Choose a feature that uniquely stands out right away, a feature that provides you with a hook to hang a picture of his name.

THE 9-11 EFFECT

Before I explain the last letter "A" in detail, which will GLUE the picture you created to the location you selected, I want you to understand just how powerful "Out of the Ordinary" images are to remembering someone's name.

Let me illustrate:
I do not remember what I did on September 10th nor what I did on September 12th but I remember the smallest details of September 11th, 2001. I remember how gorgeous the weather was that Tuesday. The cloudless, blue skies and comfortable, warm temperatures. I remember what I was doing when I first heard that a plane hit into the Twin Towers and even what I wore that day. Almost every hour is imprinted in my memory as the events unfolded. I treated patients in the afternoon who walked across the 59th St. Bridge from the financial district to get home because the trains and buses were suspended and I remember the approximate time they walked into the office. I can still see the powdery dust that covered their clothes from the tower's collapse and wiping down the tables afterwards because they were covered with it too.

I remember these small details that would have otherwise gone unnoticed and long forgotten because of an "Out of the Ordinary" attack on our country only 15 miles away. It also became the day the country would never forget. Permanently imprinted to our memories because of unimaginable events.

I relay this story to impress upon you how important

"Unusual
and
Out of the Ordinary Images"

are to enhancing your memory. You'll be using your imagination more from here on in your learning.

A Stands for ACTION

Finally, we come to the end of the P-P-A-L acronym, the letter A. I kept it for last because it is the GLUE or a strong epoxy that cements the PICTURE (created by their name) to the LOCATION, their UFF. It's critical that you bind these two together. It allows you to SEE their name on their face when you meet them next.

43

It's like gluing a post-it note to their face that only you can read every time you look at them. Mastering this last part will allow their name to come rushing back into your memory.

The letter A stands for ACTION. You are about to mentally visualize the PICTURE you created to associate with their name, perform an action at the LOCATION of their UFF.

For example, when you meet someone with the name CHRIS, immediately convert their name into a CROSS. If his UFF is a BEARD then create an ACTION connecting the crosses to his beard, such as CROSSES shooting out of his BEARD or CROSSES on fire in his beard or using a cross to groom his beard or crosses growing in his beard. The image is meant to be ABSURD. It's the 9-11 effect. The more outlandish the action, the more likely you'll remember it and the easier it will be to "See" in your mind's eye every time you meet him. It works! Ask memory enthusiasts and corporate professionals I've taught. You only need to practice using your imagination.

When you meet someone with the name Bill, convert his name into dollar bills. If you choose the lines on their face as their UFF, see money flying out of them like an ATM machine gone berserk. This creates ACTION & MOVEMENT, which GLUES the image of their name to this location. You're intent is to CEMENT them together so it triggers an image that calls up their name again, again and again. The objective is to make all actions, in your mind's eye, ABSURD, SILLY, NONSENSICAL and ILLOGICAL.

When you meet someone named Joe or Joseph, convert their name to a "Cup of Joe", maybe a Starbucks Venti Latte. Then scan their face to identify a UFF. Let's say he has flared ears, if you visualize a cup of coffee ON his flared ears without action, it's easily forgettable when trying to remember at a later time. However, if steaming hot coffee shoots out of his ears, splashing and hitting others in the face, it would create a 9-11 effect and be much more memorable.

A picture with ACTION is more likely to permanently cement it to their face. It requires some INVENTIVENESS on your part to create pictures doing absurd yet memorable actions, but you'll amaze yourself with what you can do when you persist. Be consistent and strengthen your imagination every day by hanging pictures of names on the faces of everyone you meet. I know you can do it. It only requires making a commitment to keep trying. The added benefit you'll have is the inner chuckle over the absurd images you come up with.

Let's go over a few more examples: You've just met a man named CARL who has bushy eyebrows. Convert his name to CAR (any car – a Porsche or a red Ferrari with a deep sounding vroom when you step on the gas). Visualize the Ferrari running over his eyebrows or two Ferraris racing toward one another or many Ferraris coming out of his eyebrows as though his eyebrows were garage doors opening up. This requires conceptualizing it in your mind's eye to create an association between the name Carl and his eyebrows with an absurd action involving a car.

When I was first introduced to TOM I noticed he had dimpled cheeks. The picture I used for the name Tom was TOM TOMS or DRUMS. I saw in my mind's eye drumsticks hitting his cheeks as though they were drums. Now when I look at TOM I see drum sticks beating on his cheeks and I immediately think of his name TOM.

I was introduced to a Sales Supervisor named BRUNO. I converted his name into BROOM. His unique facial feature was the top of his baldhead. I quickly visualized the following three

45

scenarios: a broom sweeping the top of his head, a broom hitting him over the head and the top of his head opening up and brooms shooting out of it. The last one was the most memorable to me and was the version I went with.

Similarly, when you meet someone named Carol or Caroline convert their name to CHRISTMAS CAROLERS. Now, create an action where you visualize in your mind's eye Christmas carolers popping out of their facial feature singing, "The First Noel" or "Rudolf the Red Nosed Reindeer." Make it funny. Make it absurd.

You've just met a woman named Denise. Convert her name into TENNIS and imagine she's hitting balls with a tennis racket that's protruding from her facial feature or a tennis racket is hitting her UFF as though it were a tennis ball.

Whenever I meet someone named John, I immediately convert their name to a toilet (going to the john.) Then I visualize an overflowing toilet spewing water from his unique facial feature.

If you meet a woman named Mary or Marie convert her name to a BRIDE getting MARRIED. If she has full lips visualize her catching a bouquet of flowers with her lips or holding a bouquet of flowers in her lips or pulling out a bridal dress from between her lips, maybe she is holding the bridal dress from her lips as the bride is looking it over.

These examples and many more will work as long as you can visualize it and make it funny, silly and unusual. Make the image unique and memorable. Give it the 9-11 Effect.

A NOTE TO THE LOGICAL & ANALYTICAL

Conjuring up mental images of unusual actions to act as TRIGGERS to remember a name doesn't come easily to many of us. I know. As a doctor for over 35 years I've dealt with facts and analysis most of my adult life; not fantasy and imagination. Blood reports, x-rays, MRIs and detailed examinations provided me with credible information to make a diagnosis and formulate a treatment plan. At my core, I am logical. So when it came to using my imagination I honestly was not the best at it; however, if you want to improve your memory to remember names and many other things, you need to develop your ability to visualize extraordinary actions in your mind's eye that are unusual and different. That's actually the BIG secret to improving your memory. Seeing a cross growing out of someone's beard would be strange to another person if you told them, so don't. It's your secret that allows you to remember their name. They'll always wonder how you were able to recall so much. Be patient with yourself and consistently use it on everyone you meet.

LET'S REVIEW THE ACRONYM P-P-A-L

You're at a business conference and you're introduced to a friend's partner, associate or boss. Perhaps you own your own business and are attempting to remember all your client's names.

P PAY ATTENTION and focus on "Hearing" their name. Avoid getting distracted by the events going on around you and GET THEIR NAME! Listen for it as you're being introduced. From experience I know this is easier said than done so be diligent with this first step. Nothing else will matter if you miss it, and if you do, ask them for their name again.

P Immediately convert their name into a PICTURE. Familiarize yourself with name conversions listed in chapter 10.

L While chatting with them, scan their face and pick a unique facial feature (LOCATION) that stands out to you right away. It could be a goatee, a scar, a mole, the size of their nose, lips, lines around their eyes, unique hairstyle or hairline. This is the location where you'll hang and glue the picture of their name.

A Create an unusual ACTION that's memorable and absurd USING the picture of their name at the location you selected. Make sure it's a little wacky and outrageous to make it STICK. Don't forget to keep it to yourself.

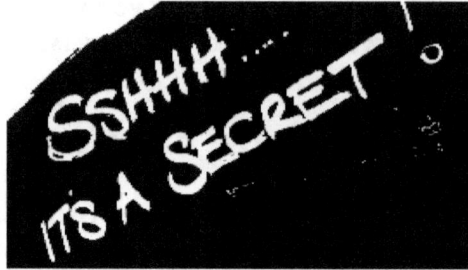

Together, let's go through another example:

(P) You've just been introduced to JIM

(P) Convert his name into an object you would find at a GYM such as a barbell or someone flexing their bulging bicep muscles.

(L) Then scan Jim's face to locate a unique facial feature. Let's say he has a prominent mustache.

(A) Quickly associate an action of a strong man to the mustache, such as the strong man RIPPING the mustache off his lip. Yeow!! But you would remember his name was Jim.

PRACTICE MAKES PERFECT

You have GREATNESS inside of you. If I could, I would wave a wand to give you an immediate ability to remember names but only you can let that greatness out! Practice and time are the keys to learning how to quickly convert names into pictures. Be persistent and you'll be rewarded for your efforts.

This is how you're going to do it. Every morning at breakfast, while reading the newspaper, scan the pictures of unknown people. Then go through the process described above. Converting their name into a picture, locating a unique facial feature and GLUEING the two with an absurd action. When you finish the paper, go back over the pictures you practiced on and say their name out loud.

Your P-P-A-L will help you remember their names and reinforce your skills every morning with only a local newspaper, a cup of coffee and a breakfast sandwich. There's no need to take any time out of your day and here's the good thing about this; it doesn't cost you anything. You don't have to set aside time out of your day to learn names. You can simply do it while you're engaged in another activity. You can remember the names of TV interview guests. You can ask all the people you meet today, the guy who makes your morning breakfast sandwich, the cashier at the store and the person at the kiosk where you buy your morning paper. You get the point. From here on in you'll create relationships with everyone you meet. Every waiter, every colleague, every employee you interact with, everyone in order to practice, practice, PRACTICE!

There's an old saying,

> ***Better to be prepared***
> ***and not have an opportunity***
> ***Than to have an opportunity***
> ***and not be prepared.***

By applying these techniques and making them a part of your every day practice, you'll be ready when it's most important – when you meet a significant person at a conference, a restaurant, the airport or at a social or business event. Focus on their name, convert it into a picture, look for a facial feature and hang a picture on them with action. It's a powerful tool that will help you build relationships and bring successes in both your personal and professional lives. This is the same technique used by memory experts and now it's yours too. Let the Greatness Within You Shine!

ONE LAST THOUGHT

Before we leave this chapter I want to share with you a confidential key to my personal successes in remembering names. Through the years I've learned that I had better results when the images had a sexual or violent nature. That's not always true but it's common enough. Aggressive and sexual actions stick better in our mind because it's more emotional and therefore make for more memorable images. Let me emphasize again to avoid the impulse to tell someone the action you created in your mind's eye. It's not always polite conversation and could be misunderstood by others.

6

TO REMEMBER NAMES "GO TO THEIR RESCUE"

The prior chapter provided you with an in-depth understanding of how Memory Experts remember names & faces by using the acronym P-P-A-L. In this chapter you'll learn 4 simple steps that will become the whip cream and cherry on top. These steps have been repeatedly written about in business and financial publications such as *Forbes* and *The Wall Street Journal* simply because forgetting names is a common problem that can have a financial impact on your overall success.

This portion is designed to push their names deeper and deeper into the bowels of your long-term memory by relying on a system of METHODICAL REPETITION to fire up multiple areas of your brain. Methodical Repetition refers to repeatedly saying, hearing and making references to someone's name to activate more and more brain neurons, which imprint it on your memory. It's not unlike the way we used flash cards in school, as a system of repetitious Rote Memory.

The acronym you'll use next is R-S-C-W or as I prefer to call it "RESCUE." Think of it as "You're Super Hero P-P-A-L coming to your R-S-C-W." After you're long finished reading this book and putting its advice into action, I want you to remember this quick phrase to help you remember names:

Your PAL (PPAL) goes to your RESCUE (RSCW) to help you remember the names of everyone you meet.

R Stands for REPEAT

After being introduced to someone ALWAYS, ALWAYS, ALWAYS repeat their name and say it back to them – IMMEDIATELY!

This is your first step to push their name it into your long-term memory. Avoid grunting or simply nodding in recognition of each other. I've personally witnessed this type of greeting too many times and it makes my hair go on fire. It's a missed opportunity to develop relationships and reinforce their name. As you now know, Names Are POWERFUL and using them can give you a HUGH EDGE in business. It's no wonder why many have difficulty remembering names... but not you. Instead, you'll echo their name back to them, "Lou, it's nice to meet you," or "Hi, Lou," or "Lou, welcome to our group."

Again, I'm often surprised how many people miss this effortless opportunity to bolster their name recognition right out of the box. It's an easy layup and a gimmee you don't want to miss. Avoid saying, "Nice to meet you." and instead insert their name at the beginning, "Maryanne, it's nice to meet you." "Mrs. Schwartz, what a pleasure to meet you." "Mr. Cooke, thank you for inviting me." Always, leading your comment with their name, which to me denotes greater respect.

After IMMEDIATELY saying their name back to them, your next step is to repeat their name at least twice more during the course of your conversation; but be warned:

DO NOT ABUSIVELY REPEAT THEIR NAME.

If someone obsessively said my name Jacqueline, Jacqueline, Jacqueline over the course of a few minutes, my antenna would go up and I would wonder what their motives were. Simply follow this adage: **Use it. Don't Abuse it!**

ASK A QUESTION

Someone introduces themself as Hank. Because you're paying attention you promptly convert their name to a picture of a BANK, visualizing the bank you frequently go to.

While scanning for a unique facial feature you repeat his name for the first time, "Hank, it's nice to meet you."

Then you **ask a question**, which allows you to repeat his name for a second time and exchange information, "Hank, how do you know the host and hostess?" or "Hank, how do you know the bride and groom?" or "Hank, what brings you to this networking event today?" or "Hank, what's your line of work?" You get the point. The question will provide you with another opportunity to repeat their name back to them.

SAYING GOODBYE

Your next easy opportunity to repeat their name and force it into your long-term memory is when you're saying goodbye or leaving for other parts of the party or event. "Bye Hank. We'll catch up later," or "It was a pleasure meeting you Hank," or "I look forward to meeting you at the July event Hank." Or "I'm leaving Hank and wanted to say goodbye." By this point, you've had at least four opportunities to say their name back to them.

Here is a list of Opportunities to REPEAT someone's name you just met:

1. Upon immediately meeting them, "Hi Betty. It's nice to meet you."

2. Right afterward in the form of a question, "Betty, how long have you worked for the company?"
3. Interjected during the course of conversation at least once more. Additional times if your conversation is longer.
4. Upon saying goodbye, "I have to go Betty but I enjoyed meeting you. Let's talk soon about making a deal between our companies. I'll call you Betty. Bye."

As I've said before, the caveat to repeating names is not to abuse and overuse them. This will defeat your ultimate purpose and may be construed as suspicious. Instead, use this opportunity to develop relationships that could lead to future business deals.

S Stands for SPELL IT

After your initial introduction and reply, now's the time to "Ask them how they spell their name."

Remember that each of these 4-steps is designed to reinforce, push, cajole, plunge and shove their name further and further into your long-term memory. It also provides an opportunity to look at them closely so you can locate a Unique Facial Feature to hang your picture. Take every opportunity to repeat their name when you can. Asking them how to spell their name is one of them.

If someone told me their name was Catherine I would say, "Catherine, it's so nice to meet you. Let me ask you, is Catherine spelt with a C or a K?"

Or, "Ann, it's a pleasure to meet you. Is Ann spelt with an E at the end or not?"

"Diane, wonderful to meet you. Do you spell your name with one N or two?"

If I met someone named Jameel I would say, "Hi Jameel, it's a pleasure. Is Jameel spelt J-a-m-e-e-l or J-a-m-e-l-e?"

"Bob, I've heard so many nice things about you. You're name is easy to spell both forward and backwards."

If their name is simple to spell like Ed or Dan I prefer to spell it out loud to reinforce it for myself. For example, "Dan, it's nice to meet you. What an easy name to spell D-A-N." Or "That's easy, R-O-N." Again this offers another nail in the coffin to reinforce their name and transfer it into your long-term memory.

There are times when it's not appropriate to ask them how they spell their name. One of those times is when you're introduced to many people at once.

Let's say I'm attending an office event and someone I know calls out, "Jacqueline, come meet the group who handles acquisitions and mergers. He then starts going around the group, introducing them without allowing me to go through the usual steps we've been reviewing. "This is Jim, Tom, Nyesha, Raja and Jill."

The time to go through your steps has just shortened. First things first - repeat their name back to them and identify a Facial Feature. I usually say, "Very nice to meet you all" and proceed to shake each of their hands while repeating their names as discussed in step one, "Jim, nice to meet you. (Picturing a Strong Man at the Gym) Tom, a pleasure. (Picturing Drums) Nyesha, I heard about your successes last year (Picturing I'll eat ya) Raja, always a pleasure, (Picturing a Dodger Baseball player) and Jill, (Picturing a Pill). You're a very seasoned crew. Nice to meet you all." Later, when given a chance to speak to them privately, I'll ask them how they spell their name to reinforce it into my memory.

C Stands for COMMENT ON THEIR NAME

After you've REPEATED their name out loud and asked how to SPELL it, NOW it's time to COMMENT on their name to push it further into your long-term memory.

Earlier we discussed that a name is not a rose by any other name. A person's name encompasses their individuality, their ego and their identity. For all intent and purposes, IT IS THEM!! Their name is part of their soul. Their name is part of their heart and needs to be HANDLED WITH CARE because who they are is encapsulated in their name.

With that in mind, when you tell someone their name is beautiful they often brighten up because it's interpreted as THEY ARE beautiful. I'm not a psychologist nor am I pretending to be one but I do know patients and have over 35 years of seeing how words have a healing effect on us. People will directly associate you with having said nice things about them, even though you only commented on their name.

Therefore, when commenting on someone's name it makes sense to COMPLIMENT only and AVOID, AVOID, AVOID any criticism. Let me say it another way and imagine my arms waving up and down as a warning:

CAUTION – FRAGILE - HANDLE NAMES WITH CARE!!

Even if you feel a joke brewing in your mind or they have a name that inspires one-liners, jest and jabs –DON'T DO IT. It is never OK to mock someone's name. Let me repeat that –

IT IS NEVER OK TO TAUNT, TEASE OR INSULT SOMEONE'S NAME

One culture's DeShawn is another culture's Sophia. A name often reflects cultural origins and is often given as a badge of pride and a symbol of ancestry. Then there are those names given as a tribute to another family member, possibly a name from a generation long gone, a name that's no longer "cool."

I had a secretary whose last name was BUTT. She wasn't proud to carry her family name because as a kid she was the butt of many jokes. She legally changed her name when she turned 18, taking control of how she wanted the world to perceive her.

Let's remember that people will interpret a "beautiful name" comment as saying they're beautiful but they'll also interpreted jeers, jokes and wisecracks as criticism against them. What you think is a joke they've heard since they were young, over and over again. Kids can be cruel and your joke could be yet another reminder of all the times they had been ridiculed. AVOID IT, AVOID IT, AVOID IT!! You can't predict how people will respond. Don't do it and let your better angels prevail. Better yet, teach this to the young people in your life to prevent name teasing going forward. The last thing you want to do is unintentionally insult someone when you're trying to build a relationship of RESPECT. Giving a positive comment about their name is icing on the cake.

I've met many people with unusual names I can hardly pronounce and they'll tell me, "Oh, just call me Steve or Jenny." Others will take me syllable by syllable so I can pronounce it properly. Whatever they prefer, I'll do as they ask.

As we've discussed, calling someone by name opens the door to building relationships based on respect. Relationships you can harvest and grow into either doing direct business or as a bird dogs who carries your business card and refers friends, family and coworkers to you. People prefer to do business with people they know, like and trust. In their mind, they already have a relationship with you that can be further developed with time.

Here's a list of comments I frequently use. Feel free to add your own:

- That's a powerful name.
- What culture is your name from?
- What a beautiful name.
- Such a sweet name.
- What do you prefer to be called?
- Were you named after your Father?
- Is that a family name passed down through the generations?

Let's Review:

- You walk into an event with a FOCUSED ATTENTION to hear the names of everyone you meet and tune out distractions.
- After being introduced, you immediately convert their name into a PICTURE.
- And promptly REPEAT their name saying, "(NAME) It's nice to meet you,"
- Then you LOCATE a unique facial feature.
- In your mind's eye you give the picture an ACTION at their UFF, making it memorable and unusual.
- Then ask, "How do you spell your name?" or "Is your name spelt (spell name)?"
- Then make a comment, "Tom, is that a family name?" or "Is your father also named Thomas?"

You've paid attention, converted their name into a picture, located a unique facial feature, created an action, repeated their name, spelt it and made a comment in less than 30 seconds. You're on your way to accomplishing my goal for you...to be able to remember the name of everyone you meet.

W *Stands for WRITE DOWN THEIR NAME*

Last but not least, if you meet someone who's important enough to NOT forget their name, the last letter of the R-S-C-W acronym will come to your rescue. W refers to WRITE IT DOWN.

To REINFORCE their names, purchase a small notebook to record the triggers you created – the pictures you CONVERTED their names into, unique facial features and their jobs. There are lined pages in the back of this book for you to write down those names. Here's how I record them:
- Elaine; VP of Sterling Bank; dimpled cheeks; eating in a bowling lane.
- John; attorney; receding hairline; toilet overflowing.
- Bruno; sales manager; bald; top of head opens and brooms fly out.

Everywhere you go, refer to your notebook. After a meeting, office event, neighborhood party or after casually meeting someone while shopping; jot it down while it's fresh in your mind. Then review their names and triggers regularly as you add more; during a coffee break, while sitting on the toilet, when in line at the post office, bank or at a red light. You get the point. It doesn't need to be scheduled but instead multitasked. Years ago I read the entire third book of Harry Potter while waiting for red lights to turn green in NY City. Hey, it was better than getting upset everyday.

So, when your body is occupied doing one thing and your mind is free to engage in another, that's the time to review your names and their triggers. If you see a name in the newspaper or hear one on television, note the picture that comes to your mind. For example, I associate the Monopoly Money Bags Guy in black tails and top hat with the name Richie, Rich or Richard. You may have another image. Begin with the names you're familiar with then expand onto others. When I meet anyone with the name Ted, I picture a bed. If he has a beard or bushy eyebrows I associate people sleeping in a bed in his beard or imagine a bed over each eye. A woman named Karen has a mole on her cheek. I convert Karen to carrots and see carrots shooting out of her mole. At first you'll write down everyone's name and after you're more comfortable, only those you don't want to forget or unusual names you come across.

Be patient. You'll get better and faster soon enough, especially if you're using the newspaper every morning. In the mean time, enjoy the process and the exaggerated images you're creating in your mind's eye.

As I said before, "It's better to be prepared and not have an opportunity rather than have an opportunity and not be prepared." You WILL be ready my friends if you follow these few steps. And why is that important?

Because people prefer to do business with those they know rather than people they don't.

It's then up to you to determine the course of your reputation and the depth of the relationship you build.

If you own your own business and are determined to remember all your customer's name when they enter your restaurant, store, salon or shop - writing them down will help you achieve your goal very quickly. By using the 8-steps we reviewed in the last 2 chapters and sending your super hero pal to your rescue, you'll amaze your customers, build loyalty and develop new business relationships along the way.

SUMMARY

R = Repeat their name.
- Immediately say their name back to them
- Use several times during conversation
- Ask a question that repeats their name
- Use to say goodbye
- Remember to - Use it; don't abuse it.

S = Spell their name.
- Ask, "How is that spelt?"
- "Oh, that's easy to spell M-A-R-Y,"
- Avoid asking when introduced to more than one person at a time

C = Comment on their name.
- Make positive comments about their name
- Avoid making jokes about a name.

W = Write it down
- Record and review the names of people you meet
- Write down their line of work, job titles, pictures and triggers you created

7 ZIP NAMES & LAST NAMES

When you hear the word ZIP you may have an image of a speeding bolt of lightening crossing your path or perhaps the term "In a Flash" comes to mind. Descriptors like Streak, Dart, Brisk, Sprint and Rush all denote fast action and energy. So fast in fact that it's difficult to SEE the details of what just ZIPPED by.

Now imagine a flash of sound whipping by; faster than an ambulance siren or police wail because there's no fading echo in the distance. If it's hard for your eyes to notice details when something is MOVING FAST, it's even harder for your brain to interpret what you HEARD when it's said in a fraction of a second and possibly against competing sounds.

ZIP NAMES are just that...they're "faster than a speeding bullet."

Uncommon first names and most last names can whisk right by your audible comprehension. They are names that are easily and often forgotten.

Think of it like the Star Ship Enterprise disappearing from the sky at warp speed. Now it's here and now it's – POOF – gone! No remnant trails to follow. No trace to give you a clue where it originated. ZIP NAMES also leave no clues or fading echo to reinforce them.

They are the most abstract of names and therefore are difficult to transform into pictures because we have little to no prior experience or built-up contextual association with them. For example, if you're introduced to someone named MARK, you may already know a Mark from another job or from school or you know an athlete, celebrity, musician or even a close friend or family member named Mark. There are references you can pull at from your past knowledge of MARKs to the person standing in front of you. However, when you meet someone named Osaka or Callum you may not have an immediate reference in your memory to connect to their name because you rarely, if ever met someone with that name.

Cities like New York, Miami, Los Angeles, London and Paris are multicultural epicenters where international companies set up headquarters. However, today you can run an international business from a home in Topeka, Kansas or Jackson, Wyoming allowing you to reach beyond small town borders and meet people whose names don't reflect your hometown. Names like Sally, Jane and Tim will become interspersed with names like Raheem, Shaniqua and Yin. We already see it in the names of our news anchors, celebrities and sports heroes. Our exposure to unfamiliar names will become more prevalent in the near future requiring a strategy for remembering multisyllabled foreign names that otherwise would ZIP right on by.

Remembering ZIP NAMES requires that you go through the same process as previously discussed, using the two acronyms P-P-A-L and R-S-C-W in order to:

Create a picture of their name and Associate it with action to a facial feature.

It's a little more work to retain but it's worth the effort when you see the expression on their face when you not only remember their name but also pronounce it correctly. I've seen that expression many times, eyes widened, mouth open and an immediate respect for you because of the deference you paid them by remembering their name.

BREAKING DOWN COMPLICATED NAMES

People with foreign sounding and complicated names are used to having their names butchered in pronunciation or completely forgotten. That's why you'll make a big impression when you accurately pronounce and recall their name. It's harder to remember a name like Bommiraju than a name like John, so here's how you'll do it:

FIRST:

Unapologetically ASK them to repeat their name and slowly pronounce each syllable by saying, **"Could you please repeat your name slowly?"** Don't worry. They're used to being asked to repeat their name and clarify its pronunciation, especially if you're meeting them for the first time.

SECOND:

Immediately REPEAT their name back to them until you can say it to their approval. Break it down by syllables and repeat those you're not pronouncing properly until you do. Don't be shy. Who wouldn't want someone to be able to pronounce their name correctly? You're gaining favor in their eyes just by taking an interest to get their name right!

THIRD:

Create an IMAGE for each syllable. This is the best way to remember their name. Then combine them all into one final image. I understand it may sound complicated at first but with practice and time it will be second nature.

EXAMPLES

You've just been introduced to Mr. Bommiraju who's the head of sales. Break down his name into the following syllables: BOMB – EAR – AHH – SHOE. You could conjure an image of a bomb in his ear that makes him sneeze AH-AH-AHHCHOO! Or you can combine the first two syllables together and the last two syllables together to form BOMBER –AHCHOO. I'm picturing a bomber who sneezes AHHCHOO to light the fuse. You get the point. Break up the syllables into pictures and combine them into one image. It requires practice but let me assure you that in a short time you'll be able to quickly create and combine images that allow you to remember complicated names. The good thing is it doesn't cost you anything to make your client feel respected and appreciated; a respect that is can be rewarded with loyalty for a long time.

Here's another example, I was meeting an executive to discuss giving a "Remembering Names" presentation to his team. His secretary's name was Falencia. She was the gatekeeper and the appointment scheduler. Her boss, who I had an appointment with made the yes / no decision but it was Falencia who wielded the power to put my call through or to decide which day I would speak to their group. Calling her by her name created a friendlier bond more quickly than if I had not shown her the deference of learning her name. That's because the name Falencia is a Zip Name, a forgettable name that's often not remembered by others. Unconsciously she understood that people who called her by her name were "Close to Her" and thought of as family, friends and coworkers. By taking the time to remember her name and pronouncing it properly, it was easier to become associated with the "Friends and Family" category and get a good day and time for my presentation.

> 1. Let's break her name down into syllables: FALL – ENCE – SEE – AHH.

> 2. Now into individual pictures: FALL – FENCE – SEE YA.

> 3. Now into ONE image: (After) Falling off a fence (she brushes herself off and says) See Ya.

After a while, you'll forget the images you created and only her name will be left in your permanent memory.

LAST NAMES

You will use the same principles as described above when remembering last names:

1. Break down their name into its syllables.
2. Create an image for each syllable.
3. Then combine all the images into one picture.

Let's go over an example:

When you're introduced to Mr. and Mrs. Goldberg you'll break down their last name into the image of GOLD (gold coins) and BERG (iceberg). You can combine them by visualizing glimmering gold coins reflecting light off the sides of an iceberg or bags of gold littering an iceberg or it's raining gold coins over an iceberg. When you're pressured for time my advice is to go with the first image you conjure. Then repeat it in your mind's eye to reinforce the imagery, making it vivid and realistic.

You're introduced to Mrs. Kovacs. Breaking down her name into syllables you have CO - VACS. Now create images of COLD (snow) – VACUUM. Combining them into an image you may see a vacuum sucking up the snow outside or you're pulling out the vacuum from a cold freezer making it an actual Cold Vacuum. These images are simply triggers to remind you of their name. They don't have to be exact but I strongly recommend you use pictures that create the most emotional or contextual connections with that image.

PRACTICING LAST NAMES

In this section you'll have an opportunity to practice creating images for last names. Try them yourself and afterwards we'll go through them together. Be patient and stay with it. You are training your brain to think differently and strengthening your imagination to "Think Outside the Box."

Here are the stages again you'll use to remember ZIP NAMES:

1. Break down their name into its syllables.
2. Create an image for each syllable.
3. Then combine them into one image.

1.	Zielinski	6.	Schneider
2.	Malur	7.	Hoffman
3.	De Groot	8.	Kazlauskiene
4.	Rotari	9.	McMurphy
5.	Camilleri	10.	Gelashvili

Cover the bottom half of this page and go through the names using your own imagination. Following the steps described above before reading the suggestions below. You can do it!

ZIELINSKI

1. ZY – LIN – SKI
2. VIOLIN (by combining the first two syllables) – SKI
3. Violin Skiing down a mountain

MALUR

1. MA – LURE
2. MA (your Mother) – (Fishing) LURE
3. Your Mother is fishing with a Lure or your Mother is wearing fishing Lures or a fishing lure in the shape of your Mother or your Mother has a fishing lure in her mouth.

DE GROOT

1. DE – ROOT
2. DEAD – ROOT
3. Dead tree Roots are entangled in their hair or around their body.

ROTARI

1. ROW – TAR – EE
2. ROW (boat) – (hot) TAR – EAT
3. Rowing in hot Tar while eating or Rowing and Eating hot Tar. You can even see the entire name as ROTARY as though they're spinning and rotating.

CAMILLERI

1. CAMIL – AIR – EE
2. CAMEL – HAIRY (by combining the last two syllables) A Camel that's very Hairy. See hair extending from the camel's humps.

SCHNEIDER

1. SCHNY – DER
2. SLIDER (by combining both syllables)
3. Sliding down a bannister

HOFFMANN

1. HOFF – MAN
2. HUFF – MAN
3. Man Huffs and puffs and blows you down or Huffs and puffs to blow everything around in a whirlwind.

KAZLOUSKIENE

1. KAZ – LOUSE – SKEEN
2. CAT – LOUSY – SKIN
3. Cat has Lousy Skin – see in your mind's eye a hairless cat with drooping, stretched skin.

McMURPHY

1. MIC – MURF –EE
2. MICKEY (mouse) – SMURF – EAT
3. Mickey Mouse has a blue Smurf in his mouth and is eating it

GELASHVILI

1. GHEL – ASH – VEE – LEE
2. GOULASH – VILLAGE – EATS or GOULASH – LILLY (combining the two syllables and finding a word that rhymes with villy.)
3. The entire Village comes out to Eat Goulash or Goulash grows out of Lilies.

Keep practicing on names you read in the newspaper or see on TV and it goes without saying that after meeting a client with a Zip Name, write it down as soon as possible. Then break it apart into its syllables to create memorable images so you'll always have their name on the tip of your tongue when you meet them next.

New opportunities await you with your advanced skills!

8

PRACTICE WHAT YOU'VE LEARNED

Congratulations! You now have the tools to successfully remember all the names you will ever meet and although our journey together is ending soon, your quest is just beginning.

Having the ability to Remember your customer's Names is the cornerstone to a successful business because there is POWER in calling someone by their name. It represents their ego, their identity and their sense of pride. It conveys that you respect them enough, you value them enough, you care enough to take the time to remember them. It creates an opportunity to feel more connected to you, which can open doors to new relationships and potentially new prospective clients. It's a skill that will accelerate your successes in business and everyday life.

Through persistent practice, you will unleash Greatness and Potentials within you that can open doors and reinforce loyalty to current and future clients. The last step of your journey requires motivation to allow your imagination to create pictures of names! Remember the following words of wisdom:

It's better to be prepared and not have an opportunity, than to have an opportunity and not be prepared.

In this chapter you'll have the opportunity to practice the steps of P-A-L (Picture – Action – Location) and reinforce them before your next corporate event or party. As we go through it together you'll better understand how to master this effective system.

Many students have told me that the first time they used this system at a party, they were able to remember more names than without it and each time thereafter it became easier and easier until eventually they were able to call out everyone's name. When you keep your eye on the goal, with time, patience and practice so will you.

EXAGGERATE, EXAGGERATE, EXAGGERATE

Before we start, let me remind you that the more absurd and ridiculous you make your pictures the more they'll "STICK" in your memory. Give them all the 9-11 Effect. Don't worry about it being perfect, especially if you're having difficulty with a name. Your speed will improve with time and those you have trouble with, you'll write down to work on later.

WELCOME TO THE PARTY! LET'S MEET THE GUESTS

Allow me to introduce you to
Anna Vasquez.

Immediately convert Anna's name into a picture. It conjures the image of a BANANA. You may or may not decide to remember her last name when you first meet, unless she introduces herself as Mrs. Vasquez.

When her last name is broken into syllables you get: VAS - QUEZ. Then into individual pictures: FAST – QUIZ. When you put all the images together the BANANA is taking a FAST QUIZ or a FAST WHIZ. Isn't that a more memorable image?

Anna has many Unique Facial Features to choose as locations: Her hairline indent on the right side of her head, her wide nose, full bottom lip and dark eyebrows all stand out. Choose the one that holds your attention the most.

Now give your picture a memorable ACTION at the location you chose. If it's her nose, you may see bananas shooting out from her nostrils like torpedoes. If it's her lips, she may be shooting bananas out of her mouth or maybe you see her lips as actual bananas. Make it funny, make it unique, make it stand out in your mind's eye.

Allow me to introduce you to

Neil Fleming.

His first name conjures the picture of a person KNEELING. His last name sounds similar to FLAMING.

When you put both pictures together you visualize a KNEELING person in FLAMES.

Neil has a few Unique Facial Features to choose as locations: The deep lines on the side of his nose and mouth; the lines under his eyes, the thin top lip. Choose the one that holds your attention the most.

Now give your picture a memorable ACTION at your chosen location. If it's the lines on the side of his nose, you may see a man kneeling on those lines shooting flames at you. If you choose his thin upper lip you may see someone kneeling on his lips shooting flames into his nostrils or maybe you see flames shooting out as though from his mouth. Either way, your picture can easily combine both his first and last names.

Allow me to introduce you to **Susan Pearce.**

Her first name conjures the picture of a LAZY SUSAN – a turntable that holds food items. Her last name creates an image of piercing an object with a sharp pin or knife.

When you put both pictures together you can visualize piercing a Lazy Susan with a big pin or knives you would throw like darts.

Susan has a few Unique Facial Features to choose as locations: The long bangs that cover her forehead; the dark eyebrows or the thin top lip. Choose the one that holds your attention the most.

Now give your picture a memorable ACTION at your chosen location. If it's the long bangs that cover her forehead, you may see a Lazy Susan spinning in the middle of her forehead with knives or large pins being thrown at it. If you've chosen her thin upper lip you may conjure a picture of many Lazy Susans shooting out of her mouth and knives being thrown at them in mid-air to pierce them. If you choose her dark eyebrows you may see a Lazy Susan over each eyebrow, spinning and shooting out pins at everyone else to pierce them. Either way, one picture can be made that combines both her first and last names with ACTION.

Allow me to introduce you to
Rory Weston.

His first name conjures the picture of a LION ROARING. His last name sounds similar to VEST-ON.

When you put both pictures together you can visualize a ROARING LION WEARING A VEST.

Rory has a few Unique Facial Features to choose as locations: The long forehead and bald head; his wide nose; the lines on the side of his nose and mouth and slightly flared ear. Choose the one that holds your attention the most.

Now give your picture a memorable ACTION at your chosen location. If you've chosen his wide nose you can imagine a lion poking his head out of each nostril, roaring loudly while wearing a vest with the letters RW on them (his initials). If you chose the lines on the side of his nose and mouth you can picture two lions on each side of his face scratching out the lines on his face with their claws while rearing up their heads and roaring. If you choose his long forehead and bald head you may see a lion sitting on top of his head roaring loudly with his teeth showing and wearing a vest over his fur. Either way, your picture can easily combine both his first and last names with ACTION.

Allow me to introduce you to
Tony Mancusi.

His first name (TOE-KNEE) conjures the picture of a TOE sticking out of a KNEE. His last name sounds similar to MANICURE or MACCARRONI. I prefer manicure and will use it for this example.

When you put both pictures together you can visualize a TOE protruding out of a KNEE getting a MANICURE - filing the toenail or painting it with polish.

Tony has a few Unique Facial Features to choose as locations: His thick bushy eyebrows are very distinctive as well as his M-SHAPED hairline with stand-up hair. You may also be drawn to the lines (bags) under his eyes or his full bottom lip.

You'll notice he hasn't shaven and has day old growth. Unless there's a defined beard, goatee or mustache I'm not inclined to use it as a location. He may have cheeks as smooth as a baby when I meet him next. Choose the one that holds your attention the most.

Now give your picture a memorable ACTION at your chosen location. If you've chosen his bushy eyebrows or bags under his eyes you can imagine a knee with toes growing out of it giving each other manicures. If you chose his stand-up hair and M-Shaped hairline you may see toes standing tall in his hair throwing manicure files like missiles. Use what comes naturally to you as your ACTION and remember to keep your thoughts to yourself.

Allow me to introduce you to
Salome Patel.

Her first name conjures the picture of SALAMI. Imagine the ones hanging from a hook at your deli.

Her last name sounds similar to PADDLE or Flower PETAL. Flower petals are nice but they're passive objects that are seen and not actively used. Whenever you have the choice between a passive and an active

image, use the active one every time. That's why the image of a PADDLE will be the one we'll work with in this example

When you put both pictures together, you can visualize a SAMAMI being used as a PADDLE in a rowboat.

Salome has a few Unique Facial Features to choose as locations: Her hairline and hair part on her left; her rounded cheeks and full face; a jutting chin; dark eyebrows or even the deep facial lines along the side of her nose and lips. Choose the one that holds your attention the most.

Now give your picture a memorable ACTION at your chosen location. If you've chosen her rounded face and full cheeks you may see salami slices shooting from her cheeks as they're hit by a paddle; If you choose the lines on the side of her nose you may visualize the salami lying in the crease and the paddle used to cut it up into slices; If you use her hair part and left hairline you may visualize salamis coming at you like missiles that are hit away by paddles. If you choose her dark eyebrows you could see her brows as salami and paddles are hitting them. Whichever picture you choose, you'll attempt to combine both her first and last names with ACTION.

Allow me to introduce you to

Paige Walcott.

Her first name conjures the picture of a "Page from a book" or a "Page of loose leaf" or "A Page from the Royal Court." Use the image that appears first. It's most likely the strongest image of PAIGE for you.

Her last name creates an image of camping cots hanging on a wall or cots secured to the wall in their open position.

When you put both pictures together with Action you can visualize pages of paper lying on the cot and shooting out at the viewer or the cot snapping opened and closed and every time it opens it releases a rain storm of paper like it's confetti.

Close your eyes and visualize that image. When you can really see it in your mind's eye, you'll imprint it onto your memory. This is the core principle that easily allows you to remember names.

Susan has a few Unique Facial Features to choose as locations: Her slender lips; her thin eyebrows and the distinctive lines on the side of her mouth and nose. Choose the one that holds your attention the most.

Allow me to introduce you to
Rajah Anand.

His first name conjures the picture of a DODGE ball or MAHJON tiles as a trigger for RAJAH. His last name sounds similar to A NUN. It's close enough to work as a trigger for remembering his real name - Anand.

When you visualize A NUN, see her in a flowing black tunic that drapes to her ankles, her head covered in an elaborate, winged headdress. Details helps to burn it into your memory.

When you put both pictures together you may visualize a NUN throwing a dodge ball or nuns playing MAHJON.

Rajah has a few Unique Facial Features to choose as locations: his rectangular eyeglasses are very distinctive and may catch your attention right away. His warm and easy smile also stands out but when you see him again he may not be smiling. His long, dark eyebrows and full, dark hair are also personal to his look.

Now give your picture a memorable ACTION at your chosen location. If you've chosen his eyeglasses you can imagine a NUN behind the glass throwing DODGE BALLS at you or a nun is throwing dodge balls at his glasses to knock them off. If you chose his eyebrows or hair you may see a nun sitting atop them and throwing dodge balls like missiles. Use what comes naturally to you as your ACTION and as always remember to keep your thoughts to yourself.

Allow me to introduce you to
Julie Chen.

Her first name conjures the picture of JEWELRY such as bracelets, necklaces and rings. Use the image that appears first in your mind's eye. It may be an image of your favorite piece of jewelry or one you gave as a gift to a loved one.

Her last name creates two plausible images; the first being CHIN and the second one HEN. Just like the earlier example, one is a passive object meant to be seen and not actively used. That's not to say you couldn't visualize JEWELRY hanging from her CHIN but whenever you have the choice between a passive and an active image, use the active one every time. That's why the image of a HEN will be the one we'll work with in this example.

When you put both pictures together with Action you can visualize a HEN pecking at jewelry or swallowing it or wearing the jewelry or clucking and dancing with a Mr. T worth of jewelry around its neck.

Julie has a few Unique Facial Features to choose as locations: Her full bottom lip, wide nose; thin, long eyebrows, almond eyes, hair parted on her left side. Choose the one that holds your attention the most.

Now give your picture a memorable ACTION at your chosen location. If you've chosen her full bottom lip you can visualize a HEN pecking at her lip to place diamond studs along her lip. If you choose her nose you can visualize diamond necklaces hanging from her nostrils and a hen clucking and pecking at the shiny bright objects. If you chose her hair part you may see a hen decked out like Mr. T in necklaces clucking and pecking along her hair part.

Allow me to introduce you to
Steve Clark.

His first name conjures the picture of shirt SLEEVES. His last name sounds similar to CLOCK.

When you put both pictures together you can visualize a large CLOCK with shirt SLEEVES flapping in the wind.

Steve has a few Unique Facial Features to choose as locations: A noticeably receding hairline on the right side; a wide forehead; distinctive laugh lines on the side of his left eye as well as deep lines on either side of his nose and lips. You may also be drawn to the small bags under his eyes or his thin top lip. Choose the one that holds your attention the most.

Now give your picture a memorable ACTION at your chosen location. If you've chosen his receding hairline you can imagine a CLOCK pasted to his head with SLEEVES draping and flapping across his face. If you chose the lines along the side of his eyes visualize a CLOCK glued to that area with the SLEEVES flapping alongside both ears. If you choose the bags or the lines on the side of his nose you may see the CLOCK at those locations and the SLEEVES reaching out to grab people as they pass. Since you don't always have a lot of time to create your image, use what comes naturally to you as your ACTION.

Allow me to introduce you to
Delanna Washington.

Her first name breaks down to DEL – ANNA, which conjures the pictures of BELL and BANANA.

Imagine a Bell ringing back & forth and the middle striker is a hanging stalk of Bananas.

Her last name brings up images of a WASHING machine or even our first President, George WASHINGTON.

Just like the example above with the flower petals, you want to choose the image that has the most action whenever possible. In this case either one can work. Let's look at them both.

When you put both pictures together, you can visualize a WASHING machine banging back and forth as it washes bells and their bananas. (What a racket!) If you choose to use our Founding Father George Washington you can visualize President Washington in knee breeches and stockings, tricorne hat, buckled shoes and cape ringing a bell with a large stalk of bananas in it saying, "Here ye, here ye." Your personal experiences and affinities will determine which image works for you.

Delanna has a few Unique Facial Features to choose as locations: her high cheek bones are very distinctive and may catch your attention right away, as well as her wide nose, full lips and long, dark eyebrows. Her braided hair is also personal to her look.

Now give your picture a memorable ACTION at your chosen location. If you choose her braided hair you can imagine George standing on her head ringing a bell saying, "Here Ye, Here Ye," or a washing machine on her head banging back and forth as bells clang and bananas jump out from the top lid. You can apply the same image to any of the locations you choose for Delanna Washington as long as you connect them with her distinctive and unique look.

Allow me to introduce you to **Akio Kwan**.

His first name conjures the picture of A KEY. His last name sounds similar to WAND.

When you put both pictures together you can visualize using a KEY as a magic WAND, "Abracadabra!"

To burn it into your memory, personalize the KEY you're visualizing. Whether you see your house key, office key, a key to a safe or storage unit that keeps your precious items; the more connections you have to the key the more likely you are to remember his name.

Akio has a few Unique Facial Features to choose as locations: His thick, full head of hair, his almond eyes, wide nose or thin lips. You may also be drawn to his wispy eyebrows that have an unusual peak on their outer sides. Choose the one that holds your attention the most.

Now give your picture a memorable ACTION at your chosen location. If you've chosen his eyes you can imagine KEYS protruding out of them as they wave in the air and say abracadabra. If you prefer his full head of hair you may see keys atop his head waving back and forth like a magician would wave his wand to manifest or summon. If you prefer to use his wide nose as your chosen location you can see keys jutting out of his nasal cavities as they're waving like a wand to conjure, call upon or transform with magic. Use what comes naturally to you in the short amount of time you have to remember his name. As always remember to keep your thoughts to yourself.

REVIEWING NAMES

After you've been introduced to a number of people at an event, it's time to check your work and reinforce their names. Go around the room and mentally recall the names of everyone you've met. If you've forgotten any, feel free to walk up to them and ask again but this time make the pictures and action MENTALLY STICK. Give them an over-the-top, 9-11 Effect so it stays in your memory for a long time to come. Sometimes, unbeknownst to us at the time, the picture or action wasn't emotionally triggering enough and POOF it vanished.

The treatment and cure to stop forgetting names is to make the picture and action even more absurd and preposterous than before. Give it a complete overhaul and check your work later to be sure that it STUCK.

SUMMARY

I bet you came up with some pretty absurd images to help you remember their names. If you did, congratulations! That's what this exercise was designed to have you do. As I've explained before, it takes practice to build up your imagination muscles in order to quickly create pictures in your mind eye, but I have no doubt that in a short time you'll be remembering names like a Memory Expert. You'll see the difference when you put this to the test at your next get together.

Continue practicing with newspapers and on people you watch on television and the internet. Use the ACTION that comes naturally to you and as always, remember to keep your thoughts to yourself.

Below are the guests you met at the party. As you're leaving, approach each of them and say good-bye by name. Feel free to write their names in the space provided.

9

TITLES, MILITARY RANKS
& OCCUPATIONS

Whenever I lecture, someone will ask me how to connect a title or occupation to a name they're remembering. How to remember whether someone's Director of Sales or the Marketing Manager; the Vice President of the company or the CEO. In the military, officers are referred to by their rank and several occupations are also referred to by their titles first such as doctors, religious leaders and levels of the academic world.

You'll need to have a system under your belt that allows you to remember if they're a Colonel or a Lieutenant; a General or an Admiral, a Doctor or a Dean. For all intensive purposes, their rank and title is part of their name.

ADDING AN OCCUPATION TO THEIR NAME

Have you ever learned how to 3-ball juggle? Including a title, company position or occupation to someone's name is similar to juggling. You start with training your hand-eye coordination to catch one ball in the air (that's their first name), then two balls alternately (their first and last names) and when you feel comfortable with that you add THE third ball (title, rank or occupation). WOW, now you're juggling! I refer to this part of your training as - The Cherry on Top.

As a word of encouragement, if the amount of information overwhelms you at any time, insert a bookmark into the page and return to it later. Be patient with yourself as you practice remembering names. This is a journey, not a race. You may want to focus your attention to capturing their first and last names first before adding a title.

WHY WE FORGET POSITIONS & TITLES

Just as names are difficult to remember because they're ABSTACT, so too are titles, positions and ranks. Most don't conjure pictures we can hold in our mind's eye, which makes them forgettable. Then we're left asking ourselves, "Was she the Chairperson or the Manager? Was he a Colonel or a Major? Is she a Miss or a Mrs.?" Titles are fluid and non-solid allowing them to ZIP RIGHT ON BY...whoosh.

HOW TO REMEMBER POSITIONS & TITLES

The SECRET to remembering someone's position is to convert it into a picture the same way you transformed their name. Below are suggestions to HELP you easily visualize and remember them. Feel free to come up with your own pictures as you see fit.

RANKINGS OF THE U.S.ARMED FORCES	
PRIVATE	LOCK & CHAIN (To keep private)
CORPORAL	APPLE CORE
SERGEANT	BARGE
LIEUTENANT	COW MOOING (rhymes with first syllable - lieu)
CAPTAIN	BASEBALL CAP
MAJOR	MAJORETTE (cheerleader with spinning baton)
COLONEL	KERNEL OF CORN
GENERAL	STARS
ADMIRAL	ADDING MACHINE
PROFESSIONS	
DENTIST	TEETH
DOCTOR	STETHOSCOPE
PSYCHOLOGIST	LYING ON A COUCH
LAWYER	SCALES OF JUSTICE
VETINARIAN	CATS & DOGS
CARPENTER	HAMMER & NAILS
ELECTRICIAN	ELELCTRICAL SHOCK

PROFESSIONS

CHIROPRACTOR	SPINE
ACCOUNTANT	CALCULATOR
DIETITIAN	SCALE
CHEF	CHEF'S HAT
COMPUTER TECHNICIAN	COMPUTER SCREEN
PHARMACIST	PILLS
TEACHER	BLACK BOARD & POINTER
COLLEGE PROFESSOR	CAP & GOWN
MARKETING	SUPERMARKET CART
ACTOR	MOVIE CAMERA
PRODUCER	PRODUCE DEPT AT THE SUPERMARKET
STOCK BROKER	TICKER TAPE MACHINE
LAW ENFORCEMENT	BADGE & GUN
FARMER	TRACTOR
SALES	SAIL BOAT
JUDGE	GAVEL
FUNERAL DIRECTOR	CASKET
SECRETARY	TYPEWRITER
REALTOR	HOUSES

CORPORATE POSITIONS

CHAIRPERSON	CHAIR
DIRECTOR	MOVIE CLAPPER
PRESIDENT	THE OVAL OFFICE
VICE PRESIDENT	CAUGHT IN A VICE
MANAGER	"MANGIA" – EAT or BABE IN A MANGER
TREASURER	PIRATE WITH EYE PATCH
CHIEF EXECUTIVE OFFICER (CEO)	INDIAN CHIEF WITH AN X (on face)
CHIEF FINANCIAL OFFICER (CFO)	INDIAN CHIEF THROWING MONEY
CHIEF OPERATING OFFICER (COO)	INDIAN CHIEF PERFORMING A SURGICAL OPERATION
MISS	HOT CHOCOLATE -Swiss Miss
MRS.	BRIDE

After visualizing an image for their name, add another picture for their title or profession using action to reinforce and glue it to the others. It's described in more detail below.

REMEMBERING THEIR OCCUPATION

While back at the party, you're now going to remember everyone's occupation as well as their names. Let's give it a whirl.

Salome Patel is the Chief Financial Officer (CFO) of her company. The picture created for her name was <u>paddling a rowboat with salami</u>. You added ACTION to the location of your choosing; her chin or lines at the side of her nose. Now you want to imagine money raining down on top of her or imagine Ms. Patel throwing money up in the air and at people because she's in charge of the money.

Tony Mancusi is a Chef at an Italian Restaurant. The picture created for his name was <u>manicuring toes along his eyebrows</u>. Now you want to image Tony wearing a white chef's hat to cover the protruding toes or each of the toes wearing chef's hats.

Paige Walcott owns a company that manufacturers woman's clothes. The picture created for her name was <u>pages of paper flying off cots that were opening and closing</u>. Now you want to imagine those pages having pictures and sketches of women's dresses.

Rory Weston is an attorney. The picture created for his name was <u>a lion sitting on his head, roaring and wearing a vest.</u> Now imagine the lion holding the scales of justice while he's roaring or the vest that he's wearing is emblazed with the scales of justice on it.

Julie Chen is a doctor. The picture created for her name was a <u>jewelry-wearing hen that was clucking and dancing on her hair part</u>. Now you want to imagine Julie also having a stethoscope around her neck or the hen wearing a stethoscope along with Mr. T's styled jewelry.

Rajah Anand is a Computer Technician. The picture created for his name was <u>a nun throwing dodge balls into his eyeglasses</u>. Now visualize his glasses as computer screens with keyboards and the nuns are throwing dodge balls at them to break the screen so he can fix them later.

Delanna Washington is a college professor. The picture created for her name was <u>a bell with bananas inside a washing machine</u>. Now visualize graduation caps bouncing on top of the washing machines denoting that she's a professor.

Steve Clark is a Judge on the Federal Bench. The picture created for his name is <u>a clock with flapping sleeves</u> at his hairline indentation on the right. Now visualize a gavel smashing the clock into pieces as you hear in your mind, "Order in the court!"

Susan Pearce is Vice-President of a major airline. The picture created for her name was a Lazy Susan spinning at her bangs and knives being thrown to pierce it. Now visualize an airplane, with a large squeezing vice around it, flying into the Lazy Susan, along with the knives being thrown, to denote she's Vice-President of an airline.

Akio Kwan is a Vetinarian. The picture created for his name was a key waving like a wand and hearing the words "Abracadabra." Now visualize using the key/wand to convert dogs into cats, cats into dogs and people into animals to denote that he's a Vetinarian.

Anna Vasquez is a Stock Broker. The picture created for her name was a banana taking a fast wiz. Now visualize the bananas taking a fast wiz but instead ticket tape information streams out with green and red arrows depicting whether the stocks went up or down for the day.

Neil Fleming is Director of Sales of his company. The picture created for his name was a <u>kneeling person who was in flames.</u> Now visualize a sailboat sailing into the flames and the director hitting the clapboard saying, "CUT!" to denote Director of Sales.

Wonderful, you're doing it. You're juggling all these pictures together to remember their first name, last name and occupation. As you can see, it requires an unleashed imagination to allow yourself to create images in your mind's eye that are beyond realistic and outside of the box. This is the essence of the Secrets used by Memory Experts.

Now you have the tools to remember the names of everyone you'll meet along with their occupation, rank or title. Commit yourself to practice daily to unleash newfound successes and within weeks you'll astound your staff, spouse and friends with your memory. Good Luck and God Bless as you begin your journey.

10 CONVERTING NAMES INTO PICTURES

Your success requires developing an ability to convert names into pictures. In this chapter I've presented two different lists. The first is comprised of the most popular names over the last 100 years according to the U.S. Department of Social Security. [1] Listed beside each name is their corresponding picture associated with it.

This is the list you want to focus on FIRST! These are the names of individuals you're most likely to meet every day.

- Review each name over and over until you can easily conjure its picture in your mind's eye.
- Then use the secondary list, with hundreds of more names, as a reference when needed. Highlight or mark the names of people you've met.
- Add additional names not on the list as you go along to expand your memory's abilities.
- Feel free to substitute your own pictures for those provided. A personal image, with an emotional connection, makes remembering a name much easier.

Most Popular Birth Names from 1918-2017

Rank	Name MEN	Picture	Name WOMEN	Picture
1	James	Chains	Mary	Marry a Bride
2	John	Toilet	Patricia	Pat Down
3	Robert	Robot	Jennifer	Gem in Fur
4	Michael	Microphone	Elizabeth	Lizard Breath
5	William	Arrow through an Apple	Linda	Window

Rank	Name MEN	Picture	Name WOMEN	Picture
6	David	Golf Divot	Barbara	Barber
7	Richard	Monopoly's Mr. Money Bags	Susan	Lazy Susan Turntable
8	Joseph	Sip a Cup of Jo (Coffee)	Jessica	Chess Piece is Sick
9	Thomas	Drums (tom toms) at Mass	Margaret	Market Shopping Cart
10	Charles	Prince Charles	Sarah	Saran Wrap
11	Christopher	Cross with Fur	Karen	Carrot
12	Daniel	Pan Yell (at it)	Nancy	Nun Sees (has many eyes)
13	Mathew	Door Mat (at Church) Pew	Betty	Betting (at a Casino)
14	Anthony	Ants on Knee	Lisa	The Mona Lisa Painting
15	Donald	Donald Duck	Dorothy	Wizard of Oz Dorothy & Toto too
16	Mark	X Marks the Spot	Sandra	Sander
17	Paul	(Basket) Ball	Ashley	Ashes on Bee
18	Steven	Sleeves	Kimberly	Swimmer Bee
19	Andrew	Ants Drawing	Donna	Donald Duck
20	Kenneth	Hen in a Net	Carol	Christmas Carolers
21	George	Gorge on food	Michelle	Mitt catching Shells
22	Joshua	Joker (in the) Sewer	Emily	Emmy Award to a Bee
23	Kevin	Kevlar Vest – Bullet Proof	Amanda	Panda (Bear)
24	Brian	Brain	Helen	Mount St. Helen Volcano
25	Edward	Head on Wood	Melissa	Missile
26	Ronald	Clown Ronald McDonald	Deborah	Dead Boar
27	Timothy	Tin (Cans) with Tea	Stephanie	Step on Me

Rank	Name MEN	Picture	Name WOMEN	Picture
28	Jason	Blue Jay in the Sun	Laura	Laurels (in Hair)
29	Jeffrey	Chef in a Tree	Rebecca	Ray (of light on) Woodpecker
30	Ryan	Rye Bread	Sharon	Actress Sharon Stone
31	Gary	Garage	Cynthia	Cinder Block
32	Jacob	Blue Jay on Cob of corn	Kathleen	Cat Leaning
33	Nicholas	Nickel	Amy	Aiming (with a scope)
34	Eric	Ear Ache	Shirley	Shirley Temple with Big Lollipop
35	Stephen	Sleeves	Anna	Banana
36	Jonathan	Toilet Thin	Angela	Angel
37	Larry	Lasso	Ruth	Baseball's Babe Ruth
38	Justin	Justice – Judge in Robes	Brenda	Branded (with a hot poker)
39	Scott	Scott Paper Towels	Pamela	Pamela Anderson (Running on Beach)
40	Frank	Frankfurter	Nicole	Nickels in Cole
41	Brandon	Branded	Katherine	Cat wearing Ring
42	Raymond	Ray of Sunshine on a Man	Virginia	Virgin Airline
43	Gregory	Keg Eats Oar	Catherine	Cat wearing a Ring
44	Benjamin	Ben Franklin Flying a Kite	Christine	Cross carried by a Teenager
45	Samuel	Uncle Sam on a Mule	Samantha	Uncle Sam
46	Patrick	Pat (Down) & Rick (Shaw)	Debra	Dead Boar
47	Alexander	Owl with Axe & Sander	Janet	Jam in a Net
48	Jack	Car Jack	Rachel	Ray of sun on Shells
49	Dennis	Tennis	Carolyn	Christmas Carolers

Rank	Name MEN	Picture	Name WOMEN	Picture
50	Jerry	Cherry	Emma	TV Emmy Awards
51	Tyler	Tire	Maria	Sangria
52	Aaron	Arrow	Heather	Feather
53	Henry	Hen Ray (of light)	Diane	Dying Ants
54	Douglas	Dug up glasses	Julie	Jewels
55	Jose	Hose	Joyce	Dr. Joyce Brothers
56	Peter	Pumpkin Eater	Evelyn	Violin
57	Adam	Atomic Bomb	Frances	France-Eiffel Tower
58	Zachary	Sack Carry	Joan	Drone or Moan
59	Nathan	Nathan's Hot Dogs	Christina	Cross carried by a Teen
60	Walter	Walt Disney	Kelly	Jelly Beans
61	Harold	Hair in Rollers	Victoria	Victory Pose with Arms In the air
62	Kyle	Tile	Lauren	Clothes Designer Ralph Lauren
63	Carl	Car	Martha	Martha Stewart
64	Arthur	Art (Picture Frame) in Fur	Judith	Shoe in a Dish
65	Gerald	Chair Cold	Cheryl	Chair is Ill
66	Roger	Walkie-Talkie "Roger that"	Megan	May Pole with Cans
67	Keith	Teeth	Andrea	Ants in a dryer
68	Jeremy	Cherry on Knee	Ann	Ants
69	Terry	Terry Cloth Towel	Alice	Owl with Lice
70	Lawrence	Lawrence Welk Orchestra Conductor	Jean	Jeans (see your favorite pair)
71	Sean	Yawn Loudly	Doris	Door w Superman S or actress Doris Day
72	Christian	Catholics Attending Mass	Jacqueline	Jack-O-Lantern Pumpkin
73	Albert	Owl & (Big) Bird	Kathryn	Cat wearing Ring
74	Joe	Cup of Jo (coffee)	Hannah	Hand Nun
75	Ethan	Eat Thin (Mints)	Olivia	Olives

Rank	Name MEN	Picture	Name WOMEN	Picture
76	Austin	Oar Tin (Can)	Gloria	Singer Gloria Estephan
77	Jesse	Chess (Piece)	Marie	Marry (Bride)
78	Willie	Eat in a Well	Teresa	Terry Cloth Towel
79	Billy	Eat Dollar Bills	Sara	Saran Wrap
80	Bryan	Brain	Janice	Jam with Lice
81	Bruce	Bruce Springsteen	Julia	Jewel Eats Ya
82	Jordan	Michael Jordan	Grace	(Back or Knee) Brace
83	Ralph	Raft	Judy	Shoe Bee
84	Roy	Santa's Toy	Theresa	Terry Cloth Towel
85	Noah	Ark with Animals	Rose	Rose
86	Dylan	Dill (Pickle) Ants	Beverly	Beverage
87	Eugene	Hugh Jeans	Denise	Dentist
88	Wayne	Weather Vane	Marilyn	Marilyn Monroe
89	Alan	Allen Wrench	Amber	Amber Stone
90	Juan	Wand	Madison	Screaming Mad at the Sun
91	Louis	Glue wrists	Danielle	Pan Yell
92	Russell	Bus has Sails	Brittany	Brittany Spears
93	Gabriel	Cab with (Fishing) Reel	Diana	Princess Diana
94	Randy	Ram into a Bee	Abigail	A Bee in Ale
95	Philip	Philip Screwdriver	Jane	Cane
96	Harry	Hairy	Natalie	Gnats & Bees
97	Vincent	Shark Fin on a Cent (penny)	Lori	Oar Eat
98	Bobby	Bobby Pins	Tiffany	Blue Box with White Ribbon
99	Johnny	Knee in Toilet	Alexis	Owl with Axe on S-Road
100	Logan	Bow on a Can	Kayla	Hay & the Law

SECONDARY LIST- FEMALE NAMES

ABBY	CAB with BEES	ALYSSA	OWL with
ABIGAIL	CABBY SAILS		MONA LISA
ABNEIGE	CAB on the		Painting
	EDGE	AMANDA	A PANDA (Bear)
ADA	AID TO HER	AMBER	AMBER Stone
	(Emergency		or HAM & BEER
	Crew)	AMELIA	AMEBA or
ADDY	Golf CADDY		Aviator AMELIA
ADELAIDE	LEMONADE		EARHART
ADELE	BRITISH SINGER	AMY	AIMING (with a
	ADELE or		Gun Scope)
	ADD a BELL	ANASTASIA	BANANA on a
ADELINE	ADD A LINE		STAGE
ADRIANNE	A TREE ANT	ANDREA	ANT DRYER
AGATHA	Author AGATHA	ANGELA	ANGEL
	CHRISTY or	ANGELINA	ANGEL
	BAG A THUG		LEANING
AGGY	BAGGY (Pants)	ANGIE	ANT BEE
AGNES	BAG NEST	ANITA	ANT EATER
ALBERTA	OWL & (Big)	ANN	ANT
	BIRD w TAR	ANNA	BANANA
ALENCIA	OWL on the	ANNABEL	BANANA BELL
	FENCE	ANNETTE	ANTS in a NET
ALEXA	OWL with AXE	ANNIE	ANTS EAT
ALEXANDRA	OWL with AXE	ANTOINETTE	ANTS TWIRL a
	& SANDER		NET
ALEXIS	OWL with AXES	APRIL	A PILL or
ALFREDA	OWL in a RED		SHOWERS &
	Dress		FLOWERS
ALICE	OWL with LICE	ARABEL	HAIRY BELL
ALICIA	OWL on a	ARIANA	HAIRY BANANA
	LEASH	ARLENE	ART LEANING
ALINE	OWL LEANING		against Wall
ALISON	Bowling ALLEY	ASHLEY	ASHES on BEE
	in the SUN	ASTRID/ASTRUD	ACID TRIP
ALTHEA	OWL having	ATHENA	City of ATHENS,
	TEA		Greece
ALVIRA	OWL with a		(PARTHENON
	VIRUS		Landmark)
		AUDREY	LAUNDRY

Name	Description	Name	Description
AUGUSTA	OAR GUST (of Wind)	BREA	FREE HER or BRIE (Cheese)
AVA	APE in a VAN	BRENDA	BRANDED (with a Hot Poker)
AYESHA	EYE EAT SHOE		
BABETTE	BAD BET	BRIDGET	BRIDGE JET
BABS	CABS or BLABS	BRITTANY	BRITTANY
BARBARA	BARBER or BARBED WIRE		SPEARS or BRITTA (Water
BEA	BUMBLE BEE		Filter) KNEE
BEATRICE	BEE doing TRICKS	BRUNHILDA	BROOM the HILL DOOR
BECKIE	DECK (of Cards) EAT	CALANDRA	CALENDAR
		CALLISTA	CALL LIST
BELINDA	BEE in a WINDOW	CAMILLE	CAMEL
		CANDICE	CAN with BEES
BELL/BELLA	BELL	CANDIDA	CANDY DOORS
BERNADETTE	BURN A NET	CARA/CARI	CAR
BERNICE	BURN KNEES	CARLA	CAR LAW
BERTHA	Give BIRTH	CARLENE	CAR LEANING
BERYL	BARREL	CARLOTTA	CAR LOT
BESS	VEST	CARLY	CAR BEE
BESSIE/BETSY	VEST EAT	CARMEL	CARAMEL (Chewy Candy)
BETH	BATH (with Rubber Ducky)	CARMELITA	CARAMEL EATER
BETHANY	BATH a KNEE		
BETHEL	BATH BELL	CARMEN	CAR (filled with) MEN
BETTINA	PATINA (on aging metals)		
		CAROL	Christmas CAROLERS
BETTY	BETTING (at a Casino)	CAROLINE	CAROLERS Hanging on a Clothes LINE
BEULAH	(Ghost) BOO LAW		
BEVERLY	BEVERY HILLS or BEVERAGE	CAROLYN	CAROLERS LINT (Roller)
BIANCA	BINACA (Breath Spray) or BEE ON CAR	CARRIE	CARRY (shopping bags)
		CASEY	(Brief) CASE EAT
BILLIE	DOLLAR BILLS EATS	CASS	CAST
		CASSANDRA	CAST SANDER
BLANCHE/BLANCHIE	(Farm) RANCH	CATHERINE	CAT wearing RING
BLYTHE	SYTHE	CATHY	CAT having TEA
BOBBIE	BOBBIE PIN	CECILE	SEE SEAL (has many Eyes)
BONNIE	BONNET		

CECILIA	SEE SEAL EAT	CLEO	CLEOPATRA
CELINA	SAIL LEANING		(Egyptian
CELINE	SINGER CELINE		Pharaoh)
	DION	CLORIS	CLAW REESES
CHARLENE	CHARRED		PIECES
	(Wood)	CLOTILDA	GLOW TILT
	LEANING		DOOR
CHARLOTTE	CHARRED	COLETTE	COAL in a NET
	(wood) in a LOT	COLLEEN	COLLIE Dog
CHELSEA	SHELLS SEE		LEANING
	(have Eyes) or	CONCHITA	CON CHEATS YA
	CHELSEA	CONNIE	CON on KNEE
	CLINTON	CONSTANCE	CON DANCING
CHERYL	CHAIR ILL	CONSTANTINE	CON STANDS
CHIQUITA	CHIQUITA		next to TEEN
	BANANA LOGO	CONSUELA	CON with
	(Woman with		SWEATER
	Basket of Fruit	CORA	(Apple) CORE
	on Head)		RAY (of Light)
CHLOE	GLOW EAT	CORDELIA	(Apple) CORE
CHRIS	CROSS		DEALS YA
CHRISSIE	CROSS SEES	CORINNE	(Apple) CORE
	(has eyes)		with RING
CHRISTIAN	CATHOLICS	CORNELIA	(Apple) CORE
	attending mass		KNEELS to EAT
CHRISTINA /CHRISTINE			YA
	CROSS carried	CORTNEY	At COURT on
	by a TEENAGER		KNEES
CICELY	SICILY, ITALY or	CRYSTAL	Quartz CRYSTAL
	SISTER on BEE	CYNTHIA	CINDER BLOCK
CINDY	CINDER BLOCK	DALE	SAIL or NAIL
CLARA	CLARINET	DALIA	DALIA FLOWER
CLARE	EGG CLAIR	DANA	HAY NUN
CLARICE	EGG CLAIRE &	DANIELLE	PAN YELL
	REECES PIECES	DAPHNE	DAPHNE DUCK
CLARISSA	EGG CLAIR &		or DEAF KNEE
	WRIST	DARLEEN	DOOR LEANING
CLAUDETTE	CLAW on DECK	DARRY	CARRY a Bag
CLAUDIA	CLAW BEE YA	DAWN	(New) BORN or
CLAUDINE	CLAW BEAN		BEAUTIFUL
CLEMENTINE	CLEMENTINE		SUNRISE
	(Tangerine-like)	DEBBIE	DEAD BEE
		DEBORAH/DEBRA	DEAD BOAR
		DEIRDRE	DEER DRYER

DELIA	DEAL YA' (Into a Card Game)	ELIZABTEH	LIZARD BREATH
DELILAH	BEE LYING with YA	ELLA	BELL LAW
DESDEMONA	DESK MOANING	ELLEN	Comedian ELLEN DEGENERIS
DENISE	DENTIST	ELLIE	BELLY
DIANA	PRINCESS DIANA	ELOISE	BELL has a LOW WHEEZE
DIANE	DYING ANTS	ELSA	BELL SAD
DINA	BEE NUN	ELSIE	BELL SEES (has Eyes)
DINAH	DINER		
DIXIE	PIXIE (Fairy)	EMILY	EMMY AWARD given to a BEE or FAMILY
DOLLY	DOLLY PARTON		
DOLORES	COLOR US (with Crayons)	EMMA	TV EMMY AWARD
DOMINIQUE	DOMINOES EAT		
DONNA	DONALD DUCK	ENID	EAT KNIT
DORA	DOOR RAY (of Light)	ERICA	EAR ACHE
		ERIN	4 LEAF CLOVER ERIN go BRAGH
DOREEN	DOOR REAM (of Paper)	ERMA	FUR on MA
DORIAN	DOOR EATS ANTS	ERNESTINE	FUR NEST TEENAGER
DORIS	DOOR WRIST or Actress DORIS Day	ESMERALDA	Green EMERALD
		ESSIE	NEST SEEs (has Eyes)
DOROTHY	WIZARD OF OZ DOROTHY & Toto Too	ESTELLE	NEST (Bank) TELLER
DOTTIE	DOTS IN TEA	ESTHER	NEST STIR
EDEN	Garden of EDEN	ETHEL	KETTLE or Anesthetic Spray ETHYL CHLORIDE
EDIE	EAT a BEE		
EDITH	EAT a DISH		
EDNA	HEAD NUN		
EDWINA	HEAD WINNER	ETTA	BETTING at a Casino
EILEEN	EYE LEANING		
ELAINE	EAT on a BOWLING LANE	EUGENIA	HUGH JEANS
		EUNICE	HUGH NIECE
ELEANOR	BELL A SNORE	EVA	A VAN
ELENA	BELL A NUN	EVANGELINE	OVEN LEANING
ELIANA	BELL EAT BANANA	EVE	NAKED ADAM & EVE
ELISE	BELL NIECE	EVELYN	VIOLIN
ELIZA	EAT a LIZARD	EVY	Poison IVY

FAITH	Singer FAITH HILL	GEORGINA	GORGE on JEANS NUN
FANNY	FANNY PACK or FAN on KNEE	GERALDINE	CHAIR COLD BEAN
FAY	HAY	GERMAINE	GERMAN or
FELICIA	BELL on a LEASH		CHAIR MANE (Lion's)
FERN	FERN Tree	GERRY	CHERRY
FIFI	FRENCH POODLE	GERTIE	FUR TEA or FLIRTY
FIONA	HE OWNS HER or MRS SHREK	GERTRUDE	FUR NUDE
		GIDGET	GADGET or
FLO	Water FLOW		SURFER GIRL
FLORA	FLORAL (Arrangement)		with Pony Tail
		GILDA	(FISH) GIL
FLORENCE	FLOOR ANTS		DOOR
FLOSSIE	Teeth FLOSS EAT	GILLIAN	PILL EATS ANTS
		GINA	JEANS NUN
FRAN/FRANCES	FRANCE = EIFFEL TOWER	GINGER	GINGER BREAD MAN
FRANCESCA	EIFFEL TOWER CHESS (Piece in a) CAR	GINNY	GIN (& Tonic on) KNEE or (Shark) FIN on
FRANCINE	EIFFEL TOWER SEEN (Has many Eyes)		KNEE
		GISELE	CHISEL
		GISELLA	CHISEL LAW
FREDA	FREEZE the DOOR	GLADYS	GLAD (Bags) KISS
FREDERICA	RED (Dress) DEER EATS CAR	GLENDA	BLENDER
		GLORIA	Singer GLORIA
FRITZIE	FRIZZY HAIR		ESTEPHAN
GABBY	GABBY & TALKATIVE	GRACE	Back or Knee BRACE
GABRIELLE	CAB (Film) REEL BELL	GRETA	BRITTA (Water Filter) or TV
GAIL	SAIL		Anchor GRETA
GAY	HAY		VAN SUSTEREN
GENEVIEVE	GENOVESE PHARMACY	GRETCHEN	RETCH (Vomit) CHIN
GEORGIA	GORGE (on Food)	GRISELDA	GREASE SAIL DOOR
GEORGIANA	GORGE on BANANAS	GUSSIE	GASSY (FARTING)
		GWENDA	HEN DOOR

GWENDOLYN	HEN DOE (a Deer) LINT (Roller)	IRIS	IRIS (Flower) or EYES on a WRIST
GWENETH	HEN NET	IRMA	FUR on MA
HANNAH	HAND NUN	ISABEL	IT'S A BELL
HARPER	HARP FUR	ISADORA	IT'S ADORABLE
HARRIET	HAIRY NET	JACINTA	JAR SEEN with TAR
HATTIE	HAT EAT		
HAZEL	HAY on a (Window) SIL	JACKIE	(Car) JACK EATs
		JACQUELINE	JACK-O-LANTERN Pumpkin
HEATHER	FEATHER		
HEDDA	HEAD DOOR		
HEDY	HEAD EAT	JAMIE	JAY (Bird) on KNEE
HEIDI	HIGH BEE		
HELEN	MOUNT SAINT HELEN VOLCANO	JAN	JAM (Jelly)
		JANE	CANE
		JANET	JAM in a NET
HELENE	HELL LEANING	JANICE	JAM with LICE
HELGA	HELL GAG	JEAN	JEANS
HENRIETTA	HEN RAY (of light) JET YA	JEANETTE	GEMs in a NET
		JEANNIE	JEANS EAT
HERMIONE	HAIR on MY KNEE	JEDIDIAHA	JET EATS the DYING
HESTER	COURT JESTER	JEN	GEMS
HILDA	HILL DOOR	JENNIFER	GEMS in FUR
HILDY	HILL BEE	JENNY	GEM EAT
HILLARY	HILLARY CLINTON	JESABEL	CHESS (Piece in a) BELL
HODA	HOLD UP	JESSICA	CHESS (Piece) SICS the CAR
HODEGARDE	HOLD a GUARD		
HOLLY	DOLL EAT	JESSIE	CHESS EAT
HOPE	ROPE	JILL	PILL
IDA	EYE DOOR	JO	Cup of COFFEE (A cup of JOE)
ILKA	ILL CAR		
ILSE	ILL at SEA	JOAN	DRONE or MOAN
IMOGENE	EMOJI on JEANS		
INA	EAT NUN	JOANNA	Cup of COFFEE BANANA
INDIRA	PIN a DEER with RAY (of Light)	JOANNE	COFFEE with ANTS
INGRID	PIN on a GRID		
IRENE	EYE RAIN	JOANNIE	Cup of Coffee ANTS EAT
IRINA	EYE RAIN on YA		
		JOCELYN	JOSTLE LINT Roller

JODE	TOAD	KAYSY	HAY SEES (has Eyes)
JODY	Cup of COFFEE (cup of Jo with) BEES	KEIRA	KIR ROYALE (Champagne & Chambord)
JOSEPHINE	Cup of COFFEE SIP BEAN	KELLY	JELLY Beans
JOY	JOY (Dish Soap) or HAPPY FACE☺	KELSEY	FELL into the SEA
		KIM	SWIM
JOYCE	VOICE or MOIST	KIMBER	Shouting "TIMBER"
JUANITA	WAND EATS TAR	KIMBERLY	SWIMMER BEE
JUDITH	SHOE in a DISH	KIRSTEN	CURSE a TENT
JUDY	SHOE BEE or JUDY GARLAND	KIT	KIT Cat Bar or First Aid KIT
JULIA	JEWEL EATs YA	KITTY	KITTEN having TEA
JULIANA	JEWEL EAT BANANA	KRISTEN	CROSS on a TENT
JULIE	JEWEL EAT	KYLIE	TILE EAT
JULIET	JEWEL EAT NET	LANA	LAVA
JUNE	MOON	LAURA	LAURELS (in Hair)
JUSTINE	JUSTICE (Judge) is a TEENAGER	LAUREN	RALPH LAUREN or OAR RUN
KÄÄREN/KAROUN	CAR RUNS	LAURETTE	OAR NET
KAREN	CARROT	LAURIE	OAR EAT
KARINA	CAR EAT NUN	LAVERNE	LAW BURN
KARINE	CAR RAIN	LAVINIA	LAVA EATS YA
KATE	GATE	LAYLA	LAY (on Floor) LAW
KATELYN	GATE LINT Roller	LEAH	PRINCESS LEAH
KATHERINE	CAT wearing a RING	LEE	BEE
KATHLEEN	CAT LEANING	LENA	BEE LEANING
KATHY	CAT having TEA	LEONORE	BEE & OAR
KATIA	CAT EATs BUGS	LESLIE	ACTOR LESLIE NEILSON
KATIE	GATE EATS	LETITIA	LETTER on a TISSUE
KATRINA	CAT in a TREE with a NUN	LETTY	LETTER EAT
KATTY	CAT TEA or Golf CADDY	LEXI	LEXUS Car EAT
KAY	HAY	LIBBY	LIP BEE
KAYLA	HAY & the LAW	LILA	EYE LAW
		LILLIAN	LILY ANTS

LINDA	WINDOW	MAGDA	RAG DOOR
LISA	The MONA LISA Painting	MAGDALENA	RAG DOOR LEANING
LIV	LIVE or DIE (A THUMBS UP)	MAGGIE	BAGGY
		MAISIE	DAISY
LIVVY	DIVVY UP (by cutting into pieces)	MALENA	MAIL LEANING
		MALVINA	MAIL BEAN
		MAMIE	MOMMY
LIZ	LIZARD	MANDY	MAN on BEE
LIZA	LIZA MANELLI	MARA	MARA LARGO or MARRY
LOIS	LOIS LANE (Superman's Girl)	MARALANEY	MARRY in a LANE & EAT
LOLA	BOLA Tie	MARCELLA	BAR CELLAR
LOLITA	BOW on a LITER Bottle	MARCY	BAR SEES (has Eyes)
LORETTA	LAW LETTER	MARGARET	MARKET Shopping Cart
LORNA	HORN NUN		
LORRAINE	LOW RAIN	MARGE	BARGE (Tug Boat)
LOTTIE	EAT a LOTTERY Ticket	MARGIE	BARGE EAT
LOUISA	GLUE WHEEZE YA	MARGOT	BAR GOAT
		MARGUERITE	MARGUERITA (in a Salt Rimmed Glass)
LOUISE	GLUE WHEEZE		
LUCIA	GLUE a SHELF		
LUCILLE	GLUE a SEAL or LUCILLE BALL	MARIA	SANGRIA
		MARIAH	PIRANAH or Singer MARIAH CARRIE
LUCINDA	GLUE CINDER Blocks		
LUCY	GLUE SEE (Bottle of Glue has Eyes)	MARIANNE	MARRY ANTS
		MARIE	MARRY or Singer MARIE OSMOND
LULU	Ballet TUTU		
LYDIA	LID EATS YA	MARILYN	MARILYN MONROE
LYNDSY	LINT (Brush) SEES (has Eyes)	MARION	MARRY a CON (In Orange Jumpsuit)
LYNNE	LINT (Brush/Roller)		
MADELEINE	MADELEINE ALBRIGHT	MARISOL	MARRY (Shoe) SOLE
MADGE	BADGE	MARISSA	MA's WRIST is SORE
MADISON	Screaming MAD at the SUN	MARJORIE	BAR JURY
MAE / MAY	MAYPOLE	MARLENE	BAR LEAN

MARSHA	MARSHMELLOW	MERYL	MERYL STREEP
MARTHA	MARTHA	MIA	KNEE YA
	STEWART	MICHELLE	MITT Catching
MARY	MARRY		SHELLS
MARY ELLEN	MARRY - ELLEN	MIEKA/ MIKA	KNEE hitting
	DEGENERIS		CAR
MARYELLENA	MARRY (Bride)	MILDRED	(Wind) MILL
	in L.A. by a NUN		RED (Dress)
MATEA	MA has TEA	MILLICENT	(Wind) MILL
	with YA		EATS a CENT
MATILDA	MA TILTS DOOR	MILLIE	(Wind) MILL
MATTIE	Door MAT EATS		EATS
MAUD	CORD	MIMI	MINI KNEE
MAURA	MORE RAY (of	MINA	KNEE NUN
	Light- Intensely	MINERVA	PIN into a
	Bright)		NERVE
MAUREEN	MORE RAIN or	MINNIE	MINNIE MOUSE
	MARINE	MIRANDA	MIRROR RAN
	(Oorah!)		into a DOOR
MAVIS	MAY (Pole) KISS	MIRIAM	MIRROR EATs
MAXINE	MAGAZINE		HAM
MAYA	MAYAN Indians	MISSY	MESSY
	of Mexico	MISTY	MISTY(Fog
MAYBEL	MAY pole BELL		around them)
	or MAYBELINE	MITZI	MITT that can
	Makeup		SEE (has Eyes)
MEG	LEG or Actress	MOLLY	MOLLY BOLT
	MEG RYAN	MONA	MOW NUN or
MEGAN/MEAGHAN			MOANER
	MAYPOLE with	MONICA	HARMONICA or
	CANS		MONOCLE
MEHITABEL	KNEE HITS A	MORNA	FUNERAL
	BELL		MOURNER
MELANIE	MELON EATS or	MURIEL	WALL MURAL
	MELODY	NADA	MADDER
MELINDA	MA's WINDOW	NADINE	HAY BEANS
MELISSA	MISSLE	NAN	NUN
MERCEDES	MERCEDES	NANCY	NUN SEES (Has
	BENZ		many Eyes)
MEREDITH	MARRY a DISH	NANETTE	NUN NET
MERET	MERIT BADGE	NAOMI	Fashion Model
	(from Scouts)		NAOMI
MERINE	MARINE Soldier		CAMPBELL
	(Oorah!)	NATALIE	GNAT & BEE

Name	Cue	Name	Cue
NEERA	NEAR a RAY (of Light)	PHILIPPA	PHILIP SCREWDRIVER
NELL	BELL	PHILLIS	FILL 'ER UP
NELLIE	BELLY	PHILOMENA	PILLOW MEANER
NICOLE	NICKLE in COAL		
NIKITA	NICKLE EAT TAR	PHOEBE	FRISBY
NIKKI	HICKEY on Neck	POLLY	DOLL EATS
NINA	KNEE NUN	PRISCILLA	ELVIS'S BRIDE
NOEL	CHRISTMAS GREATING or BOWL	PRUDENCE	GLUE DANCE
		PRUE	GLUE
		QUINCY	SQUINT TO SEE
NORA	DOOR RAY (of Light)	RACHEL	RAY (of light on a) SHELL
NOREEN	DOOR RAIN	RAQUEL	ROCK HELL
NORMA	DOOR MA	REBECCA	RAY (Light on) WOODPECKER
OCTAVIA	OCTAVES on the Piano	REGINA	RAY (of light on) JEANS
ODETTE	OWE a DEBT		
ODILIA	BOW DEALING cards to YA	RENA	RAIN
		RENATA	RAINING KNOTS
OLGA	Gymnast OLGA KORBUT	RENEE/RENNI	RAINING HAY
		RHODA	ROAD DOOR
OLIVIA	OLIVES	RHONDA	RUM (Captain Morgan) DOOR
OPAL	OPAL Stone		
OPHELIA	BOW FEELS YA	RITA	CHEETAH
PAM	SPAM	ROBERTA	ROBOT
PAMELA	PAMELA ANDERSON Running in red Bathing Suit	ROBIN	BATMAN'S SIDE-KICK
		ROCHELLE	ROW with SHELLS
PANDORA	PAN on a DOOR	ROSALIE	ROSES on BEE
PAT	PAT (DOWN at the airport)	ROSALIND/ROSALYN/ROSLYN	
			ROSE LINT (Roller)
PATRICIA	PAT (DOWN makes you) RICHER	ROSARIO	ROSARY
		ROSE/ROSA	ROSE
PATTY	HAMBURGER PATTY	ROSEMARIE	ROSE MARRY (Bride)
PAULA	Basket BALL	ROSITA	ROSE EATER
PAULINE	POLE LEANING	ROWENA	ROW WINNER
PEG	PEG LEG PIRATE	ROXANNE	ROCK ANT
PEGGY	PEG (Leg) EAT	ROZ	ROSIN (Hand Chalk)
PENELOPE	PENNY in Ear LOBE		

RUBY	BIG RED RUBY STONE	SILVIA	SILVER BEE
RUTH	Baseball's BABE RUTH	SIMONE	BEE MOANS
		SONIA	SONOGRAM
SABINA	SAD BEANS (Crying Loudly)	SOPHIA	ACTRESS SOPHIA LOREN
		SOPHIE	SOFA EAT
SABRINA	SAD DREAMS	STACY	DAISY
SADIE	HAY BEE	STELLA	CELLAR Doors
SALLY	SALAD	STEPHANIE	STEP ON ME
SALAMONE	SALAD MONEY	STERLING	STERLING
SAMANTHA	UNCLE SAM		SILVER Cutlery
SANDRA	SANDER	SUE	SEW or SUIT
SANDY	SAND EAT	SUE ANN	SEW ANTS
SAPHERIA	SAPHIRE (Gem Stone)	SUSAN	LAZY SUSAN TURNTABLE
SARAH	SARAN WRAP	SUSANNAH	SEW BANANA
SARI	SORRY (Very Apologetic)	SUSIE	SEW a Z
		SUZANNE	SUIT covered in SAND
SASHA	SASH (around waist)	SUZETTE	Crepe SUZETTE Flambé
SAUNDRA	SAUNA DRAW (Clothes) STEAMER	TABITHA	TABBY (Cat) BIT HER
SEEMA			
SELENA	SAIL LEANING	TAHNI	TAN the KNEE
SELENIS	SAIL LEANING toward US	TAMARA	TOMORROW
		TAMMY	CLAM EAT
SELMA	SELLING to MA	TARA	TAR
SHANNON	CANON	TERESA/TERRY	TERRY Cloth Towel
SHARIE/SHERRY	CHERRY		
SHARILYN	CHERRY LINT roller	TESS	TEST
		TESSY	TEST EATS
SHARON	ACTRESS SHARON STONE	THELMA	THELMA & LOISE (Car Flying over Cliff)
SHAWN/SEAN/SHAWNA			
	HORN or YAWN	THEODORA	THEATER DOOR
SHEILA	SHIELD	TIFFANY	TIFFANY (Blue Box with White Ribbon)
SHERYL	CHAIR ILL		
SHIRLY	CURLY or SHIRLY TEMPLE		
		TILDA	TILT the DOOR
SIBYL	CYMBAL	TILLIE	TILT while EATING
SIDNEY	SIT on KNEE		
SIGRID	Victoria's SECRET (Lingerie)	TINA	TEA NUN or Comedian TINA FEY

TOBY	TOE BEE	VIVIENNE/VIVIAN	
TONI	TOE KNEE		VIOLIN
TRACY	TRACE while EATING	WENDY	WINDY
		WILHELMINA	WILLOW (TREE)
TRICIA	TRASH YA		MEAN NUN
TRIXIE	BRICKS EAT	WILLA	(Italian) VILLA
TRUDY	NUDE BEE	WILMA	WILMA
TYRA	Neck TIE with RAY of light		FLINTSTONE
		WINIFRED	WINNIE THE POOH in a RED DRESS
URSULA	FUR SEW LAW (California)		
VAL/VALERIE	VALLEY GIRL	WINNIE	WINNIE THE POOH
VALENTINE	CUPID		
VANESSA	VAN NEST	XENI	GEM on a KNEE (Sounds like Jenny)
VELMA	BELL MA		
VERA	BEER RAY (of Light)	YAMISCHE	YOUNG BEACH
VERNA	FERN NUN	YASHARA	YOU SHARE
VERONICA	HARMONICA	YASMIN	GAS MAN
VICKY	VICK'S (Cough Drops) EAT	YETTA	JET HER
		YING	BLING or BADA BING
VICTORIA	VICTORY (Stance with arms overhead)	YOLANDA	YO-YO LAND
		YVETTE	CORVETTE
VIDA	LA VIDA LOCA or BEE at the DOOR	YVONNE	HEAVE ON (throw up on)
		ZARINA	CARs RAIN on NUN
VIOLA	VICTROLA		
VIOLET	AFRICAN VIOLET PLANT	ZELDA	SAIL DOOR
		ZERLINA	FUR LEANING
VIRGINIA	VIRGIN Airlines	ZOE	SEW 'E's
		ZULLI	ZOO BEE

SECONDARY NAME LIST- MALE NAMES

AARON	ARROW	ALISTAIR	Bowling ALLEY with STAIRS
ABE	APE	ALONZO	OWL ON ZOO
ABEL	CABLE	ALOYSIUS	OWL WISHES
ABNER	CAB FUR	ALVIN	ALVIN the Singing Chipmunk
ABRAHAM	LINCOLN (with Top Hat)		
ABRAM	APE BROOM	AMBROSE	HAM & ROSES
ADAM	ADAM & EVE or ATOMIC bomb	AMOS	Famous AMOS Cookies
		ANAND / ANON	A NUN
ADOLPH	DOLPHIN	ANATOLE	BANANA goes through a TOLL
ADRIAN	DRAIN or ROCKY'S GIRL FRIEND		
AHNAN	A NUN	ANDERSON	ANTLERS SUN
AL	OWL	ANDRE	ANDRE THE GIANT (Wrestler)
ALAN/ALLEN	ALLEN WRENCH		
ALBERT	OWL & (Big) BIRD	ANDREW	ANTS DRAWING
ALBERTO	OWL & (Big) BIRD or ALBERTO VO5 (Hair Gel)	ANDY	ANTS on a BEE
		ANGELO	ANGEL or ANTS on JELLO
ALBIN	OWL PIN		
ALDEN	OAR in the DEN	ANGUS	ANT GAS or a BLACK BULL
ALDOUS	OWL DUST or OLDEST		
		ANTHONY	ANTS on KNEE
ALEC	OWL LICKING	ANTON	ANTS twirling a BATON
ALEX	OWL with an AXE		
ALEXANDER	OWL with an AXE & SANDER	ARCHIBALD	ARCHER (Aiming at a Basket) BALL
ALF	(KEEBLER) ELF	ARCHIE	ARCHER
ALFIE	OWL FEED	ARI	HAIRY
ALFONZO	OWL "THE FONZE"	ARISTOTLE	HAIRY (Car) THROTTLE
ALFRED	OWL in a RED (Dress)		
		ARMAND	ARM BAND
ALGE	ALGAE in Petri Dishes	ARNOLD	ARM HOLD or Strongman ARNOLD SCHWARZENEGGER
ALGER	OWL in the JURY		
ALGERNON	OWL JURY NUN		
ALI	Bowling ALLEY or Boxer MOHAMMED ALI	ART	PICTURE FRAME
		ARTHUR	ART (PICTURE FRAME) FUR
		ASA	NASA or ASK HER

ASHER	ASH FUR
ASTED	PASSED (Out in) BED
AUBREY	OAR BRIE (Cheese)
AUGUST	OAR GUST of wind
AUGUSTINE	OAR GUST of wind TEENAGER
AUGUSTON	OAR GUST TON (Weight)
AUGUSTUS	OAR GUST Hitting US
AUSTIN	OAR TIN (can)
AVERY	AVIARY (ZOO BIRD CAGE)
AVIX	A VICKS (Cough Drop)
AXEL	(Wheel) AXEL
BAKRANI	BACK RAN KNEE
BALDWIN	BALD WINDOW
BARAK	BAR ROCK
BARNABY	BARN BEE
BARNEY	BARN KNEE
BARON	RED BARON (Flying a plane)
BARRET	PARROT
BARRY	(Bowl of) BERRIES
BART	DARTS or BART SIMPSON
BARTHOLOMEW	DART HOLLOW PEW
BARTON	BAR TON (Weight)
BASIL	Cooking Herb BASIL
BAYARD	HAY in your YARD
BEAUREGARD	BOW to the RED GUARD
BEN	PEN
BENEDICT	GENERAL BENEDICT ARNOLD
BENGI	PEN & BEE
BENJAMIN	BENJAMIN Franklin (Flying a Kite)
BENNETT	PEN NET
BENTLEY	PEN on BEE
BENNY	PEN on KNEE
BERNARD	BURN the YARD
BERNIE	BURN a KNEE
BERRY	(Bowl of) BERRIES
BERT	(BIG) BIRD
BERTRAM	(BIG) BIRD RAM
BERTRAND	(BIG) BIRD on the STAND (At Court)
BILL	DOLLAR BILLS
BILLY	EAT DOLLAR BILLS
BLAKE	RAKE
BOB	BOBBING BOUYS
BOBBY	BOBBY PIN
BORIS	BORIS BADENOUGH from Bullwinkle
BOYD	BOY
BRAD	BRAD PITT
BRADFORD	BRAD PITT in a FORD PICK UP
BRADLEY	BRAD PITT BEE
BRANDON	BRANDED
BRENDAN	BREAD DEN
BRENNAN	BREAD NUN
BRENT	BENT (Over)
BRET	BARRETT
BRIAN	BRAIN
BROCK	ROCK or BLOCK
BRODERICK	BROADER RICK (Shaw)
BRUCE	BRUISE or BRUCE SPRINGSTEEN
BRUNO	BROOM with a BOW
BUD	BUDWEISER BEER
BUDDY	BUDWEISER BEER & BEE
BURTON	BURN TON (Weight)
BYRON	TIE UP the RUM
CAESAR	JULIUS CAESAR in a Toga
CAL	COLLIE
CALHOUN	COLLIE (Howling at the) MOON
CALVIN	CALVIN KLEIN
CAMERON	CAMERA is ON
CARL	CAR
CARLOS	CAR LOST

CARTER	CAR STIR	CONSTANTINE	CON STANDs on a TEEN
CARY	CARRY (Shopping Bags)	COREY	(Apple) CORE EAT
CASPER	CASPER "THE FRIENDLY GHOST"	CORNEL	CORN BELL
		CORNELIUS	Apple CORE KNEELS to US
CECIL	SEA SEAL		
CEDRIC	RED (Dress) RICK (Shaw)	CRAIG	CRAIG'S LIST (Help Wanted)
CHAD	DAD	CURT	CURTAIN
CHANDLER	CHANDELIER	CURTIS	CURTAIN with *ITS
CHARLES	PRINCE CHARLES (Wearing a Crown)	CYRUS	SIREN
		DALE	TAIL
CHARLIE	CHARLIE BROWN	DAMIAN	HAY MINION
CHARLTON	CHARLSTON DANCE	DAMON	HAY MAN
CHASE	MACE	DAN	Frying PAN
CHATHAM	CHATTY HAM	DANIEL	PAN YELL (at it)
CHAUNCEY	Use CHALK to Draw a "C"	DANNEL	PAN NAIL
		DANNY	PAN on a KNEE
CHESTER	COURT JESTER	DANTE	DONALD DUCK PAYS
CHET	JET	DARIAN	BARIUM (Enema)
CHRIS	CROSS	DARIUS	CAR EATS US
CHRISTIAN	CATHOLICS (Attending Mass)	DARREN	CAR RUN
		DARRYL	BARREL
CHRISTOPHER	CROSS with FUR	DAVE/DAVEY	WAVE
CHUCK	DUCK	DAVID	Golf DIVOT
CLARENCE	CLARINET	DEAN	BEANS
CLARK	SUPERMAN ALIAS CLARK KENT	DENNIS	TENNIS
		DENNY	DEN KNEE
CLAUDE	CLAWED	DEREK	OIL DERRICK
CLAUDIO	CLAWED a BOW	DERREN	DEER RUN
CLAYTON	CLAY & TON Weight	DESI	DESI ARNEZ – "Babaloo…"
CLEM	PHLEGM		
CLIFFORD	CLIFF FORD (TRUCK)	DESMOND	DESK MAN
CLINT	MINT	DEVIN	DEVIL DOG Cakes
CLINTON	BILL & HILLARY CLINTON	DEVLIN	JAVLIN
		DEVON	DEER VAN
CLIVE	DIVE	De WITT	DEER WHISTLES
CLYDE	CLYDESDALE HORSE	DEXTER	POINDEXTER Genius
COLE	Black COAL	DICK	Ice PICK
COLLIN	COLUMN	DIEGO	EGGO waffle
CONRAD	CON (in Orange Jump Suit) with a ROD	DIMITRI	DEER KNEE TREE
		DIRK	DIRT
		DOM	DOM PERIGNON Champagne

DOMINICK	DOMINOES	ELISHA/ELIJAH	EAT EYES SHUT
DON/DONALD	DONALD DUCK	ELLERY	CELERY
DONNY	DONALD DUCK on a KNEE	ELLIS	ELLIS ISLAND – STATUE OF LIBERTY
DONOVAN	DONALD DUCK in a VAN	ELMER	ELMER'S GLUE
DORIAN	DOOR EAT ANTS	EMANUEL	EAT a (Medical) MANUAL
DOUG	DUG up Dirt	EMERY	EMERY BOARD (Nail File)
DOUGLAS	DUG up GLASSES		
DREW	GLUE	EMIL	APE (Wind) MILL
DUANE	DRAIN	EMMET	EMMY (Award) given to NY METS
DUDLEY	(Milk) DUDS Eaten by BEES or Actor DUDLEY MORE	ENOCH	HE KNOCKS
		ENRIQUE	HEN RICK (SHAW) CAKE
DUKE	THE DUKE JOHN WAYNE or PUKE	ENZO	IN the ZONE
DUNCAN	DUNKIN DONUTS or DUNCAN YOYOs	EPHRAIM	F on a RIM (of a car)
		ERASMUS	HARASS a MISS
DWIGHT	PRESIDENT DWIGHT D. EISENHOWER or FLIGHT	ERIC	EAR ACHE
		ERNEST	FUR NEST
		ERNIE	FUR KNEE
DYLAN	DILL (Pickle) ANTS or singer BOB DYLAN	ERROL	HAIR ROLL
		ERWIN	FUR WINS
EARL	Necklace of PEARLS	ETHAN	ETHAN ALLEN (Furniture Store) or EAT THIN (Mints)
EBENEZER	EBENEZER SCROOGE		
ED	HEAD		
EDDIE	HEAD EATS	EUGENE	HUGH JEANS
EDGAR	HEAD GUARD	EUSTANCE	HOUSTON or HUGH STANCE
EDMUND	HEAD MEN		
EDMUNDO	HEAD MOON DOUGH (Money)	EVAN	OVEN
		EVERETT	CLIMBING MOUNT EVERET
EDUARDO	HEAD has WAD of DOUGH (Money)	EZEKIAL	EAT ZIKA (MOSQUITOES) EAT an OWL
EDWARD	HEAD on WOOD		
EDWIN	HEAD WINS (Holding Trophy)	EZRA	PEZ (Dispenser) RAY
EGBERT	EGG BIRD (Bird sitting on Egg)	FELIX	FEEL a LICK
		FELIZ	FELIZ NAVIDAD or FELL NIECE
EISEN	EYE SAND		
ELBERT	BELL (Big) BIRD	FERDINAND	FUR IN HAND
ELDRED	BELL RED (Dress)	FERNANDO	FUR NUN DOUGH
ELI	EAT EYES	FINNEOUS	FIN EATS US
ELIAS	EAT & LIE to US	FLETCHER	PITCHER
ELIOT	BELL IDIOT	FOSTER	FROSTED GLASS

114

FRANCIS	EIFFEL TOWER CYST
FRANCISCO	EIFFEL TOWER CRISCO OIL
FRANK	FRANKFURTER
FRANKLIN	FRANKFURTER LINT (Brush)
FRED	RED (DRESS)
FREDDY	FREDDY KRUGER (With long nails)
FREDERICK	RED (DRESS) (Oil) DERRICK
FRITZ	FRIZZY HAIR or TV on the FRITZ
GABE	BABE (pig from movie) or CAVE
GABRIEL	CAB (Fishing) REEL
GARRETT	Choking with a GARRETT (A Thin Wire)
GARY	GARAGE
GASTON	GAS (Pump) TON (Weight)
GAVIN	GAVEL
GAYLORD	HAY - LORD & TAYLOR
GENE	JEANS
GEOFFREY	CHEF IN A TREE
GEORGE	GORGE (on Food)
GERALD	CHAIR COLD (with icicles)
GERARD	CHAIR ROD
GIANNI	JEAN ANTS EAT
GIANNO	JEAN ANTS HO
GIDEON	GIDDY UP (Horse)
GIFFFORD	LIFT a FORD (Truck)
GIL	FISH GILLS
GILBERT	FISH GILLS (big) BIRD
GILES	FLOOR TILES
GINO	JEAN HO
GLEN	BLEND
GODFREY	GOT away FREE (releasing a bird)
GODWIN	GOT a WIN
GORDIE	GORE a BEE (with a sword) or GAUDY
GORDON	GARDEN
GRAHAM	GRAHAM CRACKERS
GRANT	GRANITE STONE
GREG	KEG
GREGORY	KEG OAR EAT (Keg eats an oar)
GRIFFIN	GRIP a FIN or LION & EAGLE Creature
GROVER	4-LEAF CLOVER
GUNTHER	GUN FUR
GUS	GAS (Pump)
GUY	PIE
HADLEY	SAD BEE (Crying)
HAKEEM	HOT CREAM
HAL	HAIL STONES
HANK	HANKERCHIEF
HANS	HANDS
HARLAN	HAIR LINT (Roller)
HAROLD	HAIR in ROLLERS
HARRY	HAIRY
HARTLEY	HEART on a BEE
HARVEY	HARLEY Motorcycle or STEVE HARVEY
HECTOR	RECTOR (Priest)
HENRY	HEN RAY (of Light)
HERB	HERBS
HERBERT	HERBS on (Big) BIRD
HERMAN	HERMAN MONSTER
HERMANO	HAIRY MAN has the DOE (Lots of money)
HIRAM	PIE RAM (Ram a pie in their face)
HOMER	HOME RUN (Out of the park)
HORACE	DOOR RACE
HORATIO	DOORS doing math RATIOS or HORATIO ALGER
HOWARD	COWARDLY (LION) from Wizard of Oz
HOWIE	COMEDIAN HOWIE MANDEL

HOYT	AHOY MATIE	JEREMIAH	CHERRY (in my) HAND
HUBERT	HUGE (Big) BIRD		
HUGH	HUGE	JEREMY	CHERRY on KNEE
HUGO	HUGH GOAT	JERMAINE	CHAIR (Lion's) MANE
HUMPHREY	HUMP FREELY		
HUNTER	HUNTER (Looking through a Rifle Scope)	JEROME	CHAIR COMB
		JERRY	CHERRY
		JESS	CHESS (Piece)
HYMAN	PIE MAN	JESSIE	CHESS (Piece) EAT
IAN	EAT ANTS	JIM	GYM (Lifting Weights)
ICHABOD	STICKY BODY or ICHABOD KRAMER (Rip Van Winkle)		
		JIMMY	GYM EAT
		JOAQUIN	WOK CLEAN
IGNATIUS	FIG (makes you) NAUSEOUS	JOE	CUP OF JO (coffee)
		JOEL	BOWL
IGOR	EAT a BOAR (Wild Pig with tusks)	JOEY	KANGEROO BABY IN POUCH
INGRAM	FIN on GRAHM (Crackers)	JOHN	TOILET
		JOHNNY	KNEE in TOILET
IRA	EYE RAY (of light)	JONAH	JONAH in the Belly of a Whale
IRV	NERVE		
IRVING	NERVE WING	JONATHAN	TOILET THIN
IRWIN	FUR WIN	JORDAN	MICHAEL JORDAN
ISAAC	EYE SACK	JORGE	HORSE (in the) HAY
ISMAIL	IT'S the MAIL	JOSE	HOSE
ISRAEL	FISHING REEL	JOSEPH	SIP a Cup of JO
IVAN	EYE VAN	JOSH	"THE JOKER" with CLOWN MAKEUP
IZZY	FIZZY (Drink)		
JACK	CAR JACK	JOSHUA	JOKER in the SEWER
JACOB	Blue JAY on a corn COB	JOSIAH	COFFEE - MESSIAH
		JUAN	WAND
JAKE	RAKE	JUD	(Flower) BUD
JAMAL	JAW BALL	JUDE	GLUED
JAMEEL	JAW MEAL	JUDSON	(Flower) BUD in the SUN
JAMES	CHAINS		
JARED	JAR HEAD	JULES	JEWELS
JARVIS	JAR FIZZ	JULIAN	JEWEL EAT ANTS
JASPER	CASPER (The Friendly Ghost)	JULIO	Singer JULIO INGLESIAS
JAYSON	BLUE JAY in the SUN	JULIUS	JEWEL EATS US
JED	JET	JUSTIN	JUSTICE (Judge in Robes with Gavel)
JEFF	CHEF		
JEFFREY	CHEF IN A TREE	KATON	CAKE TON Weight
JENSEN	GEM in the SAND	KEITH	TEETH

KEN	HEN PECKING	LLOYD	ANNOYED (Irritated
KENNETH	HEN in a NET		& Bothered)
KENNY	HEN on a KNEE	LOGAN	BOW around a CAN
KENT	TENT	LON	FLAN (The Dessert)
KEVIN	KEVLAR VEST (Bullet	LONNY	FLAN EAT
	Proof)	LORNE	LAWN
KIMBALL	SWIM to the BALL	LOU	GLUE
KIRK	WORK (Out) or	LOUIE	GLUE EAT
	Star Trek Captain	LOUIS	GLUE WRISTS
	JAMES T. KIRK	LOWELL	BOW WELL
KIRON	KIR (Royale) RUN	LUCA	GLUE CAR
KOBI	COAL BEE or KOBI	LUCAS	GLUE CAST
	Beef	LUCIAN	GLUE SHIN
KURT	CURTAIN	LUDWIG	GLUE WIG
KYLE	TILE	LUKE	FLUKE FISH
LAMAR	LAW at the BAR	LUTHER	GLUE STIR
LANCE	DANCE or Long	LYLE	Bathroom TILE
	Jousting Spear	MAC	MACK TRUCK
	(LANCE)	MADDY	DADDY
LANCELOT	DANCES a LOT	MAL	MAIL
LANHEE	CAN EATS	MALCOLM	MAIL COMB or MAIL
LARRY	LASSO		COMES
LARS	MARS (with little	MANNY	MAN on KNEE
	green men)	MANUEL	(Medical) MANUAL
LAWRENCE	LAWRENCE WELK		or MAN in a WELL
	with BUBBLES &	MARCEL	PARCEL or CAR for
	BATON		SALE
LEM	PHLEGM	MARCUS	MARK an "X" on US
LEMUEL	PHLEGM at a MULE	MARIO	MARRY a HO
LEN	PEN	MARK	'X' MARKS THE SPOT
LENNY	PENNY or SINGER		on a Treasure Map
	LENNY KRAVITZ	MARMADUKE	THE GREAT DANE
LEO	LION	MARSHALL	MARSHALL'S
LEON	LEAN ON		Clothes Store
LEONARD	MR SPOCK -	MARTIN	MARTIAN
	LEONARD NIMOY	MARTY	MARTINI or PARTY
LEOPOLD	LION on a POLE	MARV	CARVE or
LEROY	BEE on a BOY		MARVELOUS
LESTER	LISTERINE	MARVIN	CARVIN'
LIAM	BEE on a HAM	MASON	MASON JARS with
LIONEL	LIONEL TRAINS or		air tight lids
	LION wearing a BELL	MASSIMO	MASSIVE BOW
LLEWELLYN	GLUE the WELL to	MATT	DOOR MAT
	the LINT Brush		

MATTHEW	DOOT MAT (at a Church) PEW
MAURICE	DOOR REECES Pieces
MAURY	DOOR EATS
MAX	MAXI PADS
MAXAMILLION	MAXI PADS with MILLION $$ inside
MAXWELL	MAXI PADS – in the WELL
MAYNARD	MAY POLE in a YARD
McCAY	PICK up the HAY
MEL	BELL
MELVIN	BELL WIND
MERV	NERVE
MEYER	OSCAR MEYER WEINER
MICHAEL	MICHAEL JACKSON or MICROPHONES
MICK/MICKEY	MICKEY MOUSE
MIGUEL	KNEE in GEL
MIKE	BIKE
MIKHAIL	MICKY MOUSE in a HAIL Storm
MILES	TILES
MILO	TIE a BOW
MILTON	(Wind) MILL – TON (Weight)
MISCHA	KNEE in a SHOE
MITCH	PITCH
MITCHELL	PITCH SHELL
MOE	MOW (the Lawn)
MOHAMMED	MOW over HAMMERS
MONROE	MAN ROW
MONTAGUE	MOUNTAIN with TAR & GLUE
MONTEL	MAN with a TAIL
MONTGOMERERY	MOUNTAIN of GUM is RUBBERY
MONTY	MAN TEA
MORGAN	SNORE into a CAN
MORRIS	MORRIS THE CAT or SNORE WRIST
MORT	WART
MORTIMER	WART on TIMBER
MORTON	WARTS on a TON (WEIGHT)
MORTY	WART in TEA
MOSES	MOSES (Parting the Red Sea)
MURPHY	FUR FEE or MURPHY OIL
MURRAY	FURRY
NAT	GNATS
NATE	BAIT (Box of Worms)
NATHAN	NATHAN HOT DOGS
NATHANIEL	NATHAN HOT DOG is an EEL
NAVEED	NUN (smoking) WEED
NED	HEAD
NEIL	KNEELING
NELSON	WRESTING MOVE - FULL NELSON
NERO	KNEE ROW- FIDDLING AT FIRE
NEVILLE	NUN DILL (PICKLE)
NEWTON	FIG NEWTON
NICHOLAS	NICKEL
NICHOLAI	NICKEL EYE
NICK	NICKEL
NIGEL	EYE GEL or NILE (River) - (Hair) GEL
NILES	THE NILE RIVER,
NITAN	KNIT TON (WEIGHT)
NOAH	ARK with ANIMALS
NORBERT	DOOR (Big) BIRD
NORM	(College) DORM
NORMAN	DOORMAN
NORTON	DOOR TON (Weight)
OGDEN	HOG DEN
OLAF	BOW LAUGHS
OLEG	BOW LEG

OLIVER	OLIVE FUR	QUENTIN	ACTOR QUENTIN
OMAR	HO MA		TARANTINO or
OREN / ORIN/ ORRIN			PRISON - SAN
	OAR RUN or OAR		QUENTIN
	RIM (TIRE)	QUINCY	SQUINT TO SEE
ORSON	OAR bathing in the	RAJ	DODGE (Ball)
	SUN	RALPH	RAFT
ORVILLE	OAR FILL	RANDALL	RAN (Into a) DOLL
OSWALD	(Wizard of) OZ is	RANDOLPH	RAN (Into a)
	WALLED (Off)		DOLPHIN
OTIS	BOW KISS	RANDY	RAN (Into a) BEE
OTTO	AUTO	RAOUL	RAY (of light)
OWEN	BOW WINS		DROOL
OZZIE	ROCKER OZZIE	RAPHAEL	RAFT FILE
	OSBOURNE	RAY	RAY of light
PABLO	(Painter) PABLO	RAYMOND	RAY of light on a
	PICASSO		MAN
PASCAL	PASS the GAL or	READE	READ (a Book) or
	(Easter) PASCAL		The Drug Store
	SEASON		'DUANE READE'
PATRICK	PAT (DOWN) & RICK	REAGAN	RAY GUN
	(SHAW)	REGGIE	REGGIE JACKSON -
PAUL	(BASKET) BALL		HOME RUN
PEDRO	PEDAL ROW		HITTER
PERCIVIL	PURSE – CIVIL	RENATO	RUN (over a) NUN'S
	(WAR)		TOE
PERCY	PURSE SEES (has	REUBEN	REUBEN SANDWICH
	eyes)		- CORN BEEF,SWISS
PETE	FEET or PEAT MOSS		& SAUERKRAUT on
PETER	PUMPKIN EATER		Rye
PETROV	PET LOVE or DOVE	REX	WRECKS (Breaks
PHIL	FILL-ER UP		everything up)
PHILIP	PHILIP	REYNOLD	REYNOLD'S WRAP –
	SCREWDRIVER		Aluminum Foil
PHINEAS	FIN EATS US	RICH / RICHARD	
PIERCE	PIERCE with a knife		MONOPOLY'S
PIERRE	PEE IN THE AIR		MR. MONEY BAGS
PRADO	PROD a BOW (with a	RICHIE	MR MONOPOLY
	stick)		WITH BAGS OF
PREET	FEET or FLEET		MONEY HE EATS
PRESCOT	PRESS A COT	RICK	RICK (SHAW)
PRESLEY	Elvis PRESLEY	RILEY	RYE BREAD on a BEE
PRESTON	PRESS A TON	ROB	ROBE
	(Weight)	ROBBIE	ROBBER MUG SHOT

ROBERT	ROBOT
ROCKY	ROCK EAT
ROD	CURTAIN ROD
RODDY	CURTAIN ROD EAT
RODERICK	CURTAIN ROD FUR RICK (SHAW)
RODNEY	CURTAIN ROD on KNEE
ROGER	WALKIE TALKIE "ROGER THAT"
ROLAND	ROW to LAND
ROLLO	DOLL with a BOW
ROLPH	RAFT or ROLFING Massage
ROMERO	ROME ARROW
RON	RUM – CAPTAIN MORGAN'S
RONALD	Clown - RONALD McDONALD
RONNIE	RUM on a KNEE or RUNNY
RONNIT	BONNET
RORY	ROAR
ROSCOE	BOSCO Chocolate Syrup
ROSS	FLOSS or BOSS
ROY	SANTA'S TOY FACTORY
RUDOLPH	REINDEER WITH RED NOSE
RUFUS	ROOF PUS
RUPERT	ROOF (Big) BIRD
RUSH	BRUSH
RUSS	BUS
RUSSELL	BUS SAIL
RYAN	RYE (Bread with) ANTS
SADDAM	SAD (Crying) DAM
SADDIQUE	SAD (Crying) DECK (of Cards)
SALEM	WITCHES
SAM	UNCLE SAM
SAMMY	UNCLE SAM EATS

SAMSON	UNCLE SAM in the SUN
SAMUEL	UNCLE SAM on a MULE
SAUL	SALT
SCHYLER	CRYER or SHYER
SCOTT	SCOTT PAPER TOWELS
SEAN	YAWN (Loudly)
SEBASTIAN	SEA CRASHES IN (Big Waves)
SERGEI	FUR in the HAY
SETH	DEATH (Skull head wearing black hooded cloak)
SEYMOUR	SEE MORE (eyes all over to see more)
SHANE	(Shoe) SHINE
SHELDON	SHELLS DONALD DUCK
SHELLEY	SHELL EAT
SHERMAN	GERMAN (Shepard)
SIBBY	SIPPY (Cup for Children)
SID	LID (of a Jar)
SIDNEY	SIT on KNEE
SILAS	(Barn) SILO
SIMON	Children's Game "SIMON SAYS"
SINCLAIR	PINS (in the Chocolate) ÉCLAIR
SOL	DOLL – BIG & GIRLY
SOLOMON	PINK SALMON
SOREN	(Rocket) SOARING (In the Air)
SPENCE	VP Mike PENCE
SPENCER	SUSPENDER
STAN/STANLEY	STANLEY STEEMER or STAND on a BEE
STEPHEN/STEVE	SLEEVES or STEVE HARVEY

STEWART	STEW has ART Floating in it	TYREL	NECK TIE with a BELL
STU	STEW	TYRESE	NECK TIE with GREASE
SY	SKY or PIE	TYRONE	NECK TIE on a DRONE
SYLVESTER	SILVER VEST or Actor SYLVESTER STALLONE (Rocky)	ULYSSES	YULE (Log to burn) FECES
SYRUS	SIREN	UMBERTO	PUMP (Big) BIRD'S TOE
TAD	TADPOLE		
TED	BED	UPTON	(Lift) UP TON (Weight)
TEDDY	TEDDY BEAR		
TERRANCE	TERRACE	URIAH	YOU'RE HIRED
TEX	TEXTING (on Phone)	VANCE	DANCE
THEO	TEETH with a BOW on them	VAUGH	HORN or PAWN
		VERGIL	FUR GEL
THEODORE	THEATER DOORS	VERNE	FERN (The Plant)
THOMAS	DRUMS (Tom Toms) at MASS	VERNON	FERN NUN
		VIC	VICKS COUGH DROP
THURSTON	THIRSTY or GILLIAN'S ISLAND THURSTON HOWELL the 3rd	VICTOR	THE VICTOR (with arms raised high)
		VIN	FIN (Shark)
		VINCE	FENCE
TIM	TIN (Can)	VINCENT	(Shark) FIN on a CENT (Penny)
TIMMY	TIN (Can) EATS		
TIMOTHY	TIN (Can with) TEA	VINNIE	FIN EAT
TOBIAS	TOE BITE ASS	VLAD	DAD
TOBY	TOE BEE	VLADAMIR	Get DAD a BEER
TODD	TODD SHOES (LOAFERS)	WALDO	WALL TOE
		WALKER	WALKER (Used by Disabled)
TOM	DRUMS (Tom Toms)		
TOMMY	TOMMY GUN	WALLACE	WALRUS
TONIO	TOE KNEE BOW or TONY the Tiger wearing a BOW	WALLY	WALL EAT
		WALT	WALT DISNEY or MALTED
TONY	TOE KNEE	WALTER	WALL STIR
TRAVIS	TRAVEL VISA	WARD	BOARD or (Hospital) WARD
TRENT	TENT or TRENCH		
TREVOR	(TIRE) TREAD (on a) DOOR	WARREN	Arrest WARRANT or WAR RUN
TRISTAN	TWISTING STAND	WAYNE	John WAYNE or Weather VANE
TY	NECK TIE or TIE (up with a rope)		
		WENDELL	WIND BELL
TYLER	TIRE	WES	NEST

WESLEY	NESTLE CHOCOLATE	WILSON	SOCCER BALL (TOM
WESTON	NEST TON (Weight)		HANKS' MOVIE)
WHITNEY	WHITNEY HOUSTON	WINSOR	WIND TORN
WILBUR	WELL BURNING	WINSTON	WIND (Lifts a) TON
WILFRED	WELL RED (DRESS)		(Weight)
WILL	WELL (with a Bucket	WINTHROP	WIND DROP
	& Rope)	WYATT	HAYATT HOTEL
WILLIS	WELL with GAS	XAVIER	AVIATOR (Pilot)
WILLARD	WELL in a YARD	YING	BLING or BADA
WILLIAM	ARROW THROUGH		BING
	AN APPLE	YURI	URINE
	(Reference to	ZACHARY	SACK CARRY
	William	ZACK	SACK
	Shakespeare)	ZEKE	GEEK or LEAK
WILLY	EAT in a WELL		

11 WRITING DOWN PERSONAL CONTACTS

Now you understand the Power behind calling someone by their name and the fuller meaning of Dale Carnegie's words,

> **"A person's name is the sweetest and most important sound in any language."**

In this section you'll write down the names of everyone you meet. This is equally as important as the other 7 steps. It will allow you to REVIEW their names and triggers again and again, to plunge it deeper and deeper into your long-term memory.

Review them daily until the entire process becomes natural. Once you have a picture for a name, you'll use the same picture every time you meet someone else with that name, making it easier and faster to transform names into images as you continue.

You'll be referring to Chapter 10 frequently to look up suggested pictures, so it makes sense to have all the information you'll need in one book. Here's a list of what you'll want to record in this section:

- **First Name**
- **Last Name**
- **Image for Name**
- **Facial Feature**
- **Action**
- **Occupation**
- **Job Title (if applicable)**

Congratulations on your newly acquired business skills to Remember the Names & Faces of everyone you meet. It will add to your future successes and make a positive and lasting impression on those you've remembered. Be consistent and persistent to practice on everyone both professionally and privately and feel free to contact me with any questions or success stories at Jacqueline@supersizedmemory.com. My best wishes to you all.

_____

_____

_____

_____

_____

_____

_____

_____

_____

_____

_____

_____

_____

_____

_____

_____

_____

12 BIBLIOGRAPHY

Chapter 2

1. "Career Coach: The Power of Using a Name" – Washington Post January 12,2014 Joyce E.A. Russell

2. "How our Names Shape Our Identity" – *The Week* 09-15-13 Michael Hedrick

3. Gold Star Widow Myesha Johnson makes her first public comments about the phone call from President Trump with George Stephanopoulos on GMA - October 23, 2017.

Chapter 3

1. " Addiction for Fun and Profit" – SLATE 11.10.17 Will Oremus

2. "How Dopamine Makes Us Human" – Psychology Today 05.13.11 Emily Deans M.D.

3. "People Do Business with People They Like" - Forbes Magazine June 28,2013 and Inc. Magazine October 30,2014.

4. "How Special is Derek Jeter? Just ask Joe Torre" - NY Post article July 14,2014

5. Sports of the Times; Jeter is still the Torres 'Little Boy' Shortstop – NY Times article May 31,1998

Chapter 4

1. Beck, Julie (March 04, 2014). Study: For Memory, Hearing Is Worse Than Seeing or Feeling. *The Atlantic*

2. Bigelow, James & Poremba, Amy (February 26,2014). Achilles' Ear? Inferior Human Short-Term and Recognition Memory in the Auditory Modality. PLOS One

3. Shepard, R.N. (1978b). The Mental Image. *American Psychologist* (33) 125–137. Probably Shepard's clearest statement of his views about the nature of imagery, its analog nature and its "second order isomorphism" to what it represents.

4. Shepard, R.N., Cooper, L.A., *et al.* (1982). *Mental Images and Their Transformations.* Cambridge, MA: MIT Press. A useful compendium of the seminal work by Shepard and his students on the *mental rotation* of images (and related phenomena).

5. Anderson, R. C. (1971). Encoding processes in the storage and retrieval of sentences. *Journal of Experimental Psychology, 91*(2), 338-340. (Students learn 2 ½ times faster when they use imagery)

*6 "The Millionaire Brain: Real Secrets of Millionaires" – Chapter 20 by Donny Lowy

Chapter 10

1. Department of Social Security website https://www.ssa.gov/OACT/babynames/decades/century.

ABOUT THE AUTHOR

Jacqueline Albright is a doctor over 35 years who began using memory strengthening techniques to quickly recall medical and patient information.

Now, she awakens Memory Skills inside her audiences and readers that help them learn faster, recall more and retain information longer. Her lectures are high energy, motivating and leave audiences with memory tools they can immediately use afterwards.   Let yourself be amazed by what your memory is capable of doing.

www.ingramcontent.com/pod-product-compliance
Lightning Source LLC
LaVergne TN
LVHW021511080426
835509LV00018B/2484